THE LIBRARY OF
_____

BOOK COVER

TITLE _____

AUTHOR _____

GENRE _____

METHOD _____ LENGTH _____

NOTES/QUOTES

BOOK COVER

TITLE _____

AUTHOR _____

GENRE _____

METHOD _____ LENGTH _____

NOTES/QUOTES

BOOK COVER

TITLE
AUTHOR
GENRE
METHOD   LENGTH
NOTES/QUOTES

BOOK COVER

TITLE
AUTHOR
GENRE
METHOD   LENGTH
NOTES/QUOTES

BOOK COVER

TITLE _____

AUTHOR _____

GENRE _____

METHOD _____ LENGTH _____

NOTES/QUOTES

BOOK COVER

TITLE _____

AUTHOR _____

GENRE _____

METHOD _____ LENGTH _____

NOTES/QUOTES

BOOK COVER

TITLE
AUTHOR
GENRE
METHOD   LENGTH
NOTES/QUOTES

BOOK COVER

TITLE
AUTHOR
GENRE
METHOD   LENGTH
NOTES/QUOTES

BOOK COVER

TITLE

AUTHOR

GENRE

METHOD   LENGTH

NOTES/QUOTES

BOOK COVER

TITLE

AUTHOR

GENRE

METHOD   LENGTH

NOTES/QUOTES

BOOK COVER

TITLE
AUTHOR
GENRE
METHOD   LENGTH
NOTES/QUOTES

BOOK COVER

TITLE
AUTHOR
GENRE
METHOD   LENGTH
NOTES/QUOTES

BOOK COVER

TITLE _____

AUTHOR _____

GENRE _____

METHOD _____ **LENGTH** _____

NOTES/QUOTES

★★★★★

BOOK COVER

TITLE _____

AUTHOR _____

GENRE _____

METHOD _____ **LENGTH** _____

NOTES/QUOTES

★★★★★

BOOK COVER

TITLE
AUTHOR
GENRE
METHOD   LENGTH
NOTES/QUOTES

BOOK COVER

TITLE
AUTHOR
GENRE
METHOD   LENGTH
NOTES/QUOTES

BOOK COVER

TITLE _____

AUTHOR _____

GENRE _____

METHOD _____ LENGTH _____

NOTES/QUOTES

BOOK COVER

TITLE _____

AUTHOR _____

GENRE _____

METHOD _____ LENGTH _____

NOTES/QUOTES

BOOK COVER

TITLE
AUTHOR
GENRE
METHOD   LENGTH
NOTES/QUOTES

BOOK COVER

TITLE
AUTHOR
GENRE
METHOD   LENGTH
NOTES/QUOTES

BOOK COVER

TITLE

AUTHOR

GENRE

METHOD   LENGTH

NOTES/QUOTES

BOOK COVER

TITLE

AUTHOR

GENRE

METHOD   LENGTH

NOTES/QUOTES

BOOK COVER

TITLE

AUTHOR

GENRE

METHOD   LENGTH

NOTES/QUOTES

BOOK COVER

TITLE

AUTHOR

GENRE

METHOD   LENGTH

NOTES/QUOTES

BOOK COVER	
	TITLE
	AUTHOR
	GENRE
	METHOD / LENGTH
	NOTES/QUOTES

★★★★★

BOOK COVER	
	TITLE
	AUTHOR
	GENRE
	METHOD / LENGTH
	NOTES/QUOTES

★★★★★

BOOK COVER

TITLE

AUTHOR

GENRE

METHOD   LENGTH

NOTES/QUOTES

BOOK COVER

TITLE

AUTHOR

GENRE

METHOD   LENGTH

NOTES/QUOTES

BOOK COVER

TITLE

AUTHOR

GENRE

METHOD   LENGTH

NOTES/QUOTES

BOOK COVER

TITLE

AUTHOR

GENRE

METHOD   LENGTH

NOTES/QUOTES

BOOK COVER

TITLE

AUTHOR

GENRE

METHOD   LENGTH

NOTES/QUOTES

BOOK COVER

TITLE

AUTHOR

GENRE

METHOD   LENGTH

NOTES/QUOTES

BOOK COVER

TITLE
AUTHOR
GENRE
METHOD   LENGTH
NOTES/QUOTES

★★★★★

BOOK COVER

TITLE
AUTHOR
GENRE
METHOD   LENGTH
NOTES/QUOTES

BOOK COVER

TITLE

AUTHOR

GENRE

METHOD   LENGTH

NOTES/QUOTES

★★★★★

BOOK COVER

TITLE

AUTHOR

GENRE

METHOD   LENGTH

NOTES/QUOTES

★★★★★

BOOK COVER

TITLE
AUTHOR
GENRE
METHOD   LENGTH
NOTES/QUOTES

BOOK COVER

TITLE
AUTHOR
GENRE
METHOD   LENGTH
NOTES/QUOTES

BOOK COVER

TITLE
AUTHOR
GENRE
METHOD   LENGTH
NOTES/QUOTES

BOOK COVER

TITLE
AUTHOR
GENRE
METHOD   LENGTH
NOTES/QUOTES

BOOK COVER

TITLE

AUTHOR

GENRE

METHOD   LENGTH

NOTES/QUOTES

BOOK COVER

TITLE

AUTHOR

GENRE

METHOD   LENGTH

NOTES/QUOTES

BOOK COVER

TITLE

AUTHOR

GENRE

METHOD   LENGTH

NOTES/QUOTES

BOOK COVER

TITLE

AUTHOR

GENRE

METHOD   LENGTH

NOTES/QUOTES

BOOK COVER

★★★★★

TITLE	
AUTHOR	
GENRE	
METHOD	LENGTH

NOTES/QUOTES

BOOK COVER

★★★★★

TITLE	
AUTHOR	
GENRE	
METHOD	LENGTH

NOTES/QUOTES

BOOK COVER

TITLE

AUTHOR

GENRE

METHOD   LENGTH

NOTES/QUOTES

BOOK COVER

TITLE

AUTHOR

GENRE

METHOD   LENGTH

NOTES/QUOTES

BOOK COVER

TITLE

AUTHOR

GENRE

METHOD   LENGTH

NOTES/QUOTES

BOOK COVER

TITLE

AUTHOR

GENRE

METHOD   LENGTH

NOTES/QUOTES

BOOK COVER

TITLE
AUTHOR
GENRE
METHOD   LENGTH
NOTES/QUOTES

BOOK COVER

TITLE
AUTHOR
GENRE
METHOD   LENGTH
NOTES/QUOTES

BOOK COVER

TITLE

AUTHOR

GENRE

METHOD   LENGTH

NOTES/QUOTES

BOOK COVER

TITLE

AUTHOR

GENRE

METHOD   LENGTH

NOTES/QUOTES

BOOK COVER

TITLE
AUTHOR
GENRE
METHOD   LENGTH
NOTES/QUOTES

BOOK COVER

TITLE
AUTHOR
GENRE
METHOD   LENGTH
NOTES/QUOTES

BOOK COVER

TITLE

AUTHOR

GENRE

METHOD   LENGTH

NOTES/QUOTES

BOOK COVER

TITLE

AUTHOR

GENRE

METHOD   LENGTH

NOTES/QUOTES

BOOK COVER

TITLE

AUTHOR

GENRE

METHOD   LENGTH

NOTES/QUOTES

BOOK COVER

TITLE

AUTHOR

GENRE

METHOD   LENGTH

NOTES/QUOTES

BOOK COVER

TITLE

AUTHOR

GENRE

METHOD   LENGTH

NOTES/QUOTES

★ ★ ★ ★ ★

BOOK COVER

TITLE

AUTHOR

GENRE

METHOD   LENGTH

NOTES/QUOTES

★ ★ ★ ★ ★

BOOK COVER

TITLE

AUTHOR

GENRE

METHOD   LENGTH

NOTES/QUOTES

★★★★★

BOOK COVER

TITLE

AUTHOR

GENRE

METHOD   LENGTH

NOTES/QUOTES

★★★★★

BOOK COVER

TITLE _____

AUTHOR _____

GENRE _____

METHOD _____ LENGTH _____

NOTES/QUOTES

BOOK COVER

TITLE _____

AUTHOR _____

GENRE _____

METHOD _____ LENGTH _____

NOTES/QUOTES

BOOK COVER

TITLE
AUTHOR
GENRE
METHOD   LENGTH
NOTES/QUOTES

BOOK COVER

TITLE
AUTHOR
GENRE
METHOD   LENGTH
NOTES/QUOTES

BOOK COVER

TITLE

AUTHOR

GENRE

METHOD   LENGTH

NOTES/QUOTES

★★★★★

BOOK COVER

TITLE

AUTHOR

GENRE

METHOD   LENGTH

NOTES/QUOTES

★★★★★

BOOK COVER

TITLE

AUTHOR

GENRE

METHOD   LENGTH

NOTES/QUOTES

BOOK COVER

TITLE

AUTHOR

GENRE

METHOD   LENGTH

NOTES/QUOTES

BOOK COVER

TITLE

AUTHOR

GENRE

METHOD   LENGTH

NOTES/QUOTES

★★★★★

BOOK COVER

TITLE

AUTHOR

GENRE

METHOD   LENGTH

NOTES/QUOTES

★★★★★

BOOK COVER

TITLE

AUTHOR

GENRE

METHOD   LENGTH

NOTES/QUOTES

BOOK COVER

TITLE

AUTHOR

GENRE

METHOD   LENGTH

NOTES/QUOTES

BOOK COVER

TITLE

AUTHOR

GENRE

METHOD   LENGTH

NOTES/QUOTES

BOOK COVER

TITLE

AUTHOR

GENRE

METHOD   LENGTH

NOTES/QUOTES

BOOK COVER

TITLE

AUTHOR

GENRE

METHOD			LENGTH

NOTES/QUOTES

BOOK COVER

TITLE

AUTHOR

GENRE

METHOD			LENGTH

NOTES/QUOTES

BOOK COVER

TITLE

AUTHOR

GENRE

METHOD   LENGTH

NOTES/QUOTES

BOOK COVER

TITLE

AUTHOR

GENRE

METHOD   LENGTH

NOTES/QUOTES

BOOK COVER

TITLE

AUTHOR

GENRE

METHOD   **LENGTH**

NOTES/QUOTES

BOOK COVER

TITLE

AUTHOR

GENRE

METHOD   **LENGTH**

NOTES/QUOTES

BOOK COVER

TITLE

AUTHOR

GENRE

METHOD   LENGTH

NOTES/QUOTES

⭐⭐⭐⭐⭐

BOOK COVER

TITLE

AUTHOR

GENRE

METHOD   LENGTH

NOTES/QUOTES

⭐⭐⭐⭐⭐

BOOK COVER

TITLE

AUTHOR

GENRE

METHOD   LENGTH

NOTES/QUOTES

★ ★ ★ ★ ★

BOOK COVER

TITLE

AUTHOR

GENRE

METHOD   LENGTH

NOTES/QUOTES

★ ★ ★ ★ ★

BOOK COVER

TITLE
AUTHOR
GENRE
METHOD   LENGTH
NOTES/QUOTES

BOOK COVER

TITLE
AUTHOR
GENRE
METHOD   LENGTH
NOTES/QUOTES

BOOK COVER

TITLE

AUTHOR

GENRE

METHOD   LENGTH

NOTES/QUOTES

★★★★★

BOOK COVER

TITLE

AUTHOR

GENRE

METHOD   LENGTH

NOTES/QUOTES

★★★★★

BOOK COVER

TITLE
AUTHOR
GENRE
METHOD   LENGTH
NOTES/QUOTES

BOOK COVER

TITLE
AUTHOR
GENRE
METHOD   LENGTH
NOTES/QUOTES

BOOK COVER

TITLE

AUTHOR

GENRE

METHOD   LENGTH

NOTES/QUOTES

BOOK COVER

TITLE

AUTHOR

GENRE

METHOD   LENGTH

NOTES/QUOTES

BOOK COVER

TITLE

AUTHOR

GENRE

METHOD   LENGTH

NOTES/QUOTES

BOOK COVER

TITLE

AUTHOR

GENRE

METHOD   LENGTH

NOTES/QUOTES

BOOK COVER

TITLE	
AUTHOR	
GENRE	
METHOD	LENGTH

NOTES/QUOTES

BOOK COVER

TITLE	
AUTHOR	
GENRE	
METHOD	LENGTH

NOTES/QUOTES

BOOK COVER

TITLE

AUTHOR

GENRE

METHOD   LENGTH

NOTES/QUOTES

BOOK COVER

TITLE

AUTHOR

GENRE

METHOD   LENGTH

NOTES/QUOTES

BOOK COVER

TITLE _____

AUTHOR _____

GENRE _____

METHOD _____ LENGTH _____

NOTES/QUOTES

★ ★ ★ ★ ★

BOOK COVER

TITLE _____

AUTHOR _____

GENRE _____

METHOD _____ LENGTH _____

NOTES/QUOTES

★ ★ ★ ★ ★

BOOK COVER

TITLE

AUTHOR

GENRE

METHOD   LENGTH

NOTES/QUOTES

BOOK COVER

TITLE

AUTHOR

GENRE

METHOD   LENGTH

NOTES/QUOTES

BOOK COVER

TITLE

AUTHOR

GENRE

METHOD　　　LENGTH

NOTES/QUOTES

★★★★★

BOOK COVER

TITLE

AUTHOR

GENRE

METHOD　　　LENGTH

NOTES/QUOTES

★★★★★

BOOK COVER

TITLE
AUTHOR
GENRE
METHOD   LENGTH
NOTES/QUOTES

BOOK COVER

TITLE
AUTHOR
GENRE
METHOD   LENGTH
NOTES/QUOTES

BOOK COVER

TITLE

AUTHOR

GENRE

METHOD   LENGTH

NOTES/QUOTES

BOOK COVER

TITLE

AUTHOR

GENRE

METHOD   LENGTH

NOTES/QUOTES

BOOK COVER

TITLE
AUTHOR
GENRE
METHOD   LENGTH
NOTES/QUOTES

BOOK COVER

TITLE
AUTHOR
GENRE
METHOD   LENGTH
NOTES/QUOTES

BOOK COVER

TITLE
AUTHOR
GENRE
METHOD   LENGTH
NOTES/QUOTES

BOOK COVER

TITLE
AUTHOR
GENRE
METHOD   LENGTH
NOTES/QUOTES

BOOK COVER

TITLE

AUTHOR

GENRE

METHOD LENGTH

NOTES/QUOTES

BOOK COVER

TITLE

AUTHOR

GENRE

METHOD LENGTH

NOTES/QUOTES

BOOK COVER

TITLE

AUTHOR

GENRE

METHOD   LENGTH

NOTES/QUOTES

BOOK COVER

TITLE

AUTHOR

GENRE

METHOD   LENGTH

NOTES/QUOTES

BOOK COVER

TITLE
AUTHOR
GENRE
METHOD LENGTH
NOTES/QUOTES

★★★★★

BOOK COVER

TITLE
AUTHOR
GENRE
METHOD LENGTH
NOTES/QUOTES

★★★★★

BOOK COVER

TITLE

AUTHOR

GENRE

METHOD   LENGTH

NOTES/QUOTES

BOOK COVER

TITLE

AUTHOR

GENRE

METHOD   LENGTH

NOTES/QUOTES

BOOK COVER

TITLE

AUTHOR

GENRE

METHOD   LENGTH

NOTES/QUOTES

★★★★★

BOOK COVER

TITLE

AUTHOR

GENRE

METHOD   LENGTH

NOTES/QUOTES

★★★★★

BOOK COVER

TITLE

AUTHOR

GENRE

METHOD   LENGTH

NOTES/QUOTES

BOOK COVER

TITLE

AUTHOR

GENRE

METHOD   LENGTH

NOTES/QUOTES

BOOK COVER

TITLE

AUTHOR

GENRE

METHOD   LENGTH

NOTES/QUOTES

BOOK COVER

TITLE

AUTHOR

GENRE

METHOD   LENGTH

NOTES/QUOTES

BOOK COVER

TITLE
AUTHOR
GENRE
METHOD   LENGTH
NOTES/QUOTES

BOOK COVER

TITLE
AUTHOR
GENRE
METHOD   LENGTH
NOTES/QUOTES

BOOK COVER

TITLE

AUTHOR

GENRE

METHOD   LENGTH

NOTES/QUOTES

BOOK COVER

TITLE

AUTHOR

GENRE

METHOD   LENGTH

NOTES/QUOTES

BOOK COVER

TITLE

AUTHOR

GENRE

METHOD   LENGTH

NOTES/QUOTES

BOOK COVER

TITLE

AUTHOR

GENRE

METHOD   LENGTH

NOTES/QUOTES

BOOK COVER

TITLE

AUTHOR

GENRE

METHOD   LENGTH

NOTES/QUOTES

★★★★★

BOOK COVER

TITLE

AUTHOR

GENRE

METHOD   LENGTH

NOTES/QUOTES

★★★★★

BOOK COVER

TITLE

AUTHOR

GENRE

METHOD					LENGTH

NOTES/QUOTES

BOOK COVER

TITLE

AUTHOR

GENRE

METHOD					LENGTH

NOTES/QUOTES

BOOK COVER

TITLE

AUTHOR

GENRE

METHOD　　　　LENGTH

NOTES/QUOTES

BOOK COVER

TITLE

AUTHOR

GENRE

METHOD　　　　LENGTH

NOTES/QUOTES

BOOK COVER

TITLE
AUTHOR
GENRE
METHOD   LENGTH
NOTES/QUOTES

★★★★★

BOOK COVER

TITLE
AUTHOR
GENRE
METHOD   LENGTH
NOTES/QUOTES

★★★★★

BOOK COVER

TITLE

AUTHOR

GENRE

METHOD   LENGTH

NOTES/QUOTES

★★★★★

BOOK COVER

TITLE

AUTHOR

GENRE

METHOD   LENGTH

NOTES/QUOTES

★★★★★

BOOK COVER

TITLE

AUTHOR

GENRE

METHOD   LENGTH

NOTES/QUOTES

★★★★★

BOOK COVER

TITLE

AUTHOR

GENRE

METHOD   LENGTH

NOTES/QUOTES

★★★★★

BOOK COVER

TITLE _____

AUTHOR _____

GENRE _____

METHOD _____ LENGTH ____

NOTES/QUOTES

★ ★ ★ ★ ★

BOOK COVER

TITLE _____

AUTHOR _____

GENRE _____

METHOD _____ LENGTH ____

NOTES/QUOTES

★ ★ ★ ★ ★

BOOK COVER

TITLE

AUTHOR

GENRE

METHOD   LENGTH

NOTES/QUOTES

BOOK COVER

TITLE

AUTHOR

GENRE

METHOD   LENGTH

NOTES/QUOTES

BOOK COVER

TITLE

AUTHOR

GENRE

METHOD   LENGTH

NOTES/QUOTES

BOOK COVER

TITLE

AUTHOR

GENRE

METHOD   LENGTH

NOTES/QUOTES

BOOK COVER

TITLE

AUTHOR

GENRE

METHOD   LENGTH

NOTES/QUOTES

★★★★★

BOOK COVER

TITLE

AUTHOR

GENRE

METHOD   LENGTH

NOTES/QUOTES

★★★★★

BOOK COVER

TITLE
AUTHOR
GENRE
METHOD   LENGTH
NOTES/QUOTES

BOOK COVER

TITLE
AUTHOR
GENRE
METHOD   LENGTH
NOTES/QUOTES

BOOK COVER

TITLE

AUTHOR

GENRE

METHOD   LENGTH

NOTES/QUOTES

BOOK COVER

TITLE

AUTHOR

GENRE

METHOD   LENGTH

NOTES/QUOTES

BOOK COVER

TITLE

AUTHOR

GENRE

METHOD   LENGTH

NOTES/QUOTES

BOOK COVER

TITLE

AUTHOR

GENRE

METHOD   LENGTH

NOTES/QUOTES

BOOK COVER

TITLE

AUTHOR

GENRE

METHOD   LENGTH

NOTES/QUOTES

BOOK COVER

TITLE

AUTHOR

GENRE

METHOD   LENGTH

NOTES/QUOTES

BOOK COVER

TITLE

AUTHOR

GENRE

METHOD   LENGTH

NOTES/QUOTES

BOOK COVER

TITLE

AUTHOR

GENRE

METHOD   LENGTH

NOTES/QUOTES

BOOK COVER

TITLE
AUTHOR
GENRE
METHOD   LENGTH
NOTES/QUOTES

BOOK COVER

TITLE
AUTHOR
GENRE
METHOD   LENGTH
NOTES/QUOTES

BOOK COVER

TITLE
AUTHOR
GENRE
METHOD   LENGTH
NOTES/QUOTES

BOOK COVER

TITLE
AUTHOR
GENRE
METHOD   LENGTH
NOTES/QUOTES

BOOK COVER

TITLE

AUTHOR

GENRE

METHOD   LENGTH

NOTES/QUOTES

★★★★★

BOOK COVER

TITLE

AUTHOR

GENRE

METHOD   LENGTH

NOTES/QUOTES

★★★★★

BOOK COVER

TITLE
AUTHOR
GENRE
METHOD   LENGTH
NOTES/QUOTES

BOOK COVER

TITLE
AUTHOR
GENRE
METHOD   LENGTH
NOTES/QUOTES

BOOK COVER

TITLE
AUTHOR
GENRE
METHOD   LENGTH
NOTES/QUOTES

BOOK COVER

TITLE
AUTHOR
GENRE
METHOD   LENGTH
NOTES/QUOTES

BOOK COVER

TITLE

AUTHOR

GENRE

METHOD   LENGTH

NOTES/QUOTES

BOOK COVER

TITLE

AUTHOR

GENRE

METHOD   LENGTH

NOTES/QUOTES

BOOK COVER

TITLE

AUTHOR

GENRE

METHOD   LENGTH

NOTES/QUOTES

⭐⭐⭐⭐⭐

BOOK COVER

TITLE

AUTHOR

GENRE

METHOD   LENGTH

NOTES/QUOTES

⭐⭐⭐⭐⭐

BOOK COVER

TITLE
AUTHOR
GENRE
METHOD   LENGTH
NOTES/QUOTES

BOOK COVER

TITLE
AUTHOR
GENRE
METHOD   LENGTH
NOTES/QUOTES

BOOK COVER

TITLE

AUTHOR

GENRE

METHOD   LENGTH

NOTES/QUOTES

BOOK COVER

TITLE

AUTHOR

GENRE

METHOD   LENGTH

NOTES/QUOTES

BOOK COVER

TITLE _____

AUTHOR _____

GENRE _____

METHOD _____ **LENGTH** _____

NOTES/QUOTES

BOOK COVER

TITLE _____

AUTHOR _____

GENRE _____

METHOD _____ **LENGTH** _____

NOTES/QUOTES

BOOK COVER

TITLE
AUTHOR
GENRE
METHOD   LENGTH
NOTES/QUOTES

BOOK COVER

TITLE
AUTHOR
GENRE
METHOD   LENGTH
NOTES/QUOTES

BOOK COVER

TITLE

AUTHOR

GENRE

METHOD   LENGTH

NOTES/QUOTES

BOOK COVER

TITLE

AUTHOR

GENRE

METHOD   LENGTH

NOTES/QUOTES

BOOK COVER

TITLE

AUTHOR

GENRE

METHOD   LENGTH

NOTES/QUOTES

BOOK COVER

TITLE

AUTHOR

GENRE

METHOD   LENGTH

NOTES/QUOTES

BOOK COVER

TITLE

AUTHOR

GENRE

METHOD   LENGTH

NOTES/QUOTES

★★★★★

BOOK COVER

TITLE

AUTHOR

GENRE

METHOD   LENGTH

NOTES/QUOTES

★★★★★

BOOK COVER

TITLE

AUTHOR

GENRE

METHOD   LENGTH

NOTES/QUOTES

BOOK COVER

TITLE

AUTHOR

GENRE

METHOD   LENGTH

NOTES/QUOTES

BOOK COVER

TITLE

AUTHOR

GENRE

METHOD   LENGTH

NOTES/QUOTES

★★★★★

BOOK COVER

TITLE

AUTHOR

GENRE

METHOD   LENGTH

NOTES/QUOTES

★★★★★

BOOK COVER

TITLE

AUTHOR

GENRE

METHOD   LENGTH

NOTES/QUOTES

★ ★ ★ ★ ★

BOOK COVER

TITLE

AUTHOR

GENRE

METHOD   LENGTH

NOTES/QUOTES

★ ★ ★ ★ ★

BOOK COVER

TITLE

AUTHOR

GENRE

METHOD   LENGTH

NOTES/QUOTES

★★★★★

BOOK COVER

TITLE

AUTHOR

GENRE

METHOD   LENGTH

NOTES/QUOTES

★★★★★

BOOK COVER

TITLE

AUTHOR

GENRE

METHOD   LENGTH

NOTES/QUOTES

BOOK COVER

TITLE

AUTHOR

GENRE

METHOD   LENGTH

NOTES/QUOTES

BOOK COVER

TITLE

AUTHOR

GENRE

METHOD   LENGTH

NOTES/QUOTES

★★★★★

BOOK COVER

TITLE

AUTHOR

GENRE

METHOD   LENGTH

NOTES/QUOTES

★★★★★

BOOK COVER

- TITLE
- AUTHOR
- GENRE
- METHOD LENGTH
- NOTES/QUOTES

★ ★ ★ ★ ★

BOOK COVER

- TITLE
- AUTHOR
- GENRE
- METHOD LENGTH
- NOTES/QUOTES

★ ★ ★ ★ ★

BOOK COVER

TITLE

AUTHOR

GENRE

METHOD   LENGTH

NOTES/QUOTES

★★★★★

BOOK COVER

TITLE

AUTHOR

GENRE

METHOD   LENGTH

NOTES/QUOTES

★★★★★

BOOK COVER

TITLE

AUTHOR

GENRE

METHOD　　　　　LENGTH

NOTES/QUOTES

★★★★★

BOOK COVER

TITLE

AUTHOR

GENRE

METHOD　　　　　LENGTH

NOTES/QUOTES

★★★★★

BOOK COVER

TITLE

AUTHOR

GENRE

METHOD   LENGTH

NOTES/QUOTES

★★★★★

BOOK COVER

TITLE

AUTHOR

GENRE

METHOD   LENGTH

NOTES/QUOTES

★★★★★

BOOK COVER

TITLE	
AUTHOR	
GENRE	
METHOD	LENGTH
NOTES/QUOTES	

★ ★ ★ ★ ★

BOOK COVER

TITLE	
AUTHOR	
GENRE	
METHOD	LENGTH
NOTES/QUOTES	

★ ★ ★ ★ ★

BOOK COVER

TITLE

AUTHOR

GENRE

METHOD   LENGTH

NOTES/QUOTES

★★★★★

BOOK COVER

TITLE

AUTHOR

GENRE

METHOD   LENGTH

NOTES/QUOTES

★★★★★

BOOK COVER

TITLE
AUTHOR
GENRE
METHOD   LENGTH
NOTES/QUOTES

BOOK COVER

TITLE
AUTHOR
GENRE
METHOD   LENGTH
NOTES/QUOTES

BOOK COVER

TITLE

AUTHOR

GENRE

METHOD LENGTH

NOTES/QUOTES

BOOK COVER

TITLE

AUTHOR

GENRE

METHOD LENGTH

NOTES/QUOTES

BOOK COVER

TITLE
AUTHOR
GENRE
METHOD   LENGTH
NOTES/QUOTES

★★★★★

BOOK COVER

TITLE
AUTHOR
GENRE
METHOD   LENGTH
NOTES/QUOTES

★★★★★

BOOK COVER

TITLE _____

AUTHOR _____

GENRE _____

METHOD _____ LENGTH _____

NOTES/QUOTES

★ ★ ★ ★ ★

BOOK COVER

TITLE _____

AUTHOR _____

GENRE _____

METHOD _____ LENGTH _____

NOTES/QUOTES

★ ★ ★ ★ ★

BOOK COVER

TITLE

AUTHOR

GENRE

METHOD   LENGTH

NOTES/QUOTES

BOOK COVER

TITLE

AUTHOR

GENRE

METHOD   LENGTH

NOTES/QUOTES

BOOK COVER

TITLE

AUTHOR

GENRE

METHOD   LENGTH

NOTES/QUOTES

BOOK COVER

TITLE

AUTHOR

GENRE

METHOD   LENGTH

NOTES/QUOTES

BOOK COVER

TITLE

AUTHOR

GENRE

METHOD   LENGTH

NOTES/QUOTES

BOOK COVER

TITLE

AUTHOR

GENRE

METHOD   LENGTH

NOTES/QUOTES

BOOK COVER

TITLE

AUTHOR

GENRE

METHOD   LENGTH

NOTES/QUOTES

BOOK COVER

TITLE

AUTHOR

GENRE

METHOD   LENGTH

NOTES/QUOTES

BOOK COVER

TITLE

AUTHOR

GENRE

METHOD   LENGTH

NOTES/QUOTES

BOOK COVER

TITLE

AUTHOR

GENRE

METHOD   LENGTH

NOTES/QUOTES

BOOK COVER

TITLE

AUTHOR

GENRE

METHOD LENGTH

NOTES/QUOTES

BOOK COVER

TITLE

AUTHOR

GENRE

METHOD LENGTH

NOTES/QUOTES

BOOK COVER

TITLE

AUTHOR

GENRE

METHOD   LENGTH

NOTES/QUOTES

★★★★★

BOOK COVER

TITLE

AUTHOR

GENRE

METHOD   LENGTH

NOTES/QUOTES

★★★★★

BOOK COVER

TITLE

AUTHOR

GENRE

METHOD　　　　LENGTH

NOTES/QUOTES

BOOK COVER

TITLE

AUTHOR

GENRE

METHOD　　　　LENGTH

NOTES/QUOTES

BOOK COVER

TITLE
AUTHOR
GENRE
METHOD   LENGTH
NOTES/QUOTES

BOOK COVER

TITLE
AUTHOR
GENRE
METHOD   LENGTH
NOTES/QUOTES

BOOK COVER

TITLE
AUTHOR
GENRE
METHOD   LENGTH
NOTES/QUOTES

BOOK COVER

TITLE
AUTHOR
GENRE
METHOD   LENGTH
NOTES/QUOTES

BOOK COVER

TITLE
AUTHOR
GENRE
METHOD   LENGTH
NOTES/QUOTES

BOOK COVER

TITLE
AUTHOR
GENRE
METHOD   LENGTH
NOTES/QUOTES

BOOK COVER

TITLE
AUTHOR
GENRE
METHOD   LENGTH
NOTES/QUOTES

BOOK COVER

TITLE
AUTHOR
GENRE
METHOD   LENGTH
NOTES/QUOTES

BOOK COVER

TITLE

AUTHOR

GENRE

METHOD   LENGTH

NOTES/QUOTES

BOOK COVER

TITLE

AUTHOR

GENRE

METHOD   LENGTH

NOTES/QUOTES

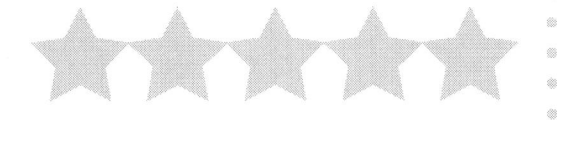

BOOK COVER

TITLE

AUTHOR

GENRE

METHOD   LENGTH

NOTES/QUOTES

BOOK COVER

TITLE

AUTHOR

GENRE

METHOD   LENGTH

NOTES/QUOTES

BOOK COVER

TITLE
AUTHOR
GENRE
METHOD   LENGTH
NOTES/QUOTES

BOOK COVER

TITLE
AUTHOR
GENRE
METHOD   LENGTH
NOTES/QUOTES

BOOK COVER

TITLE

AUTHOR

GENRE

METHOD LENGTH

NOTES/QUOTES

BOOK COVER

TITLE

AUTHOR

GENRE

METHOD LENGTH

NOTES/QUOTES

BOOK COVER

TITLE
AUTHOR
GENRE
METHOD   LENGTH
NOTES/QUOTES

BOOK COVER

TITLE
AUTHOR
GENRE
METHOD   LENGTH
NOTES/QUOTES

BOOK COVER

TITLE
AUTHOR
GENRE
METHOD   LENGTH
NOTES/QUOTES

BOOK COVER

TITLE
AUTHOR
GENRE
METHOD   LENGTH
NOTES/QUOTES

BOOK COVER

TITLE
AUTHOR
GENRE
METHOD   LENGTH
NOTES/QUOTES

BOOK COVER

TITLE
AUTHOR
GENRE
METHOD   LENGTH
NOTES/QUOTES

BOOK COVER

TITLE

AUTHOR

GENRE

METHOD   LENGTH

NOTES/QUOTES

BOOK COVER

TITLE

AUTHOR

GENRE

METHOD   LENGTH

NOTES/QUOTES

BOOK COVER

TITLE

AUTHOR

GENRE

METHOD   LENGTH

NOTES/QUOTES

BOOK COVER

TITLE

AUTHOR

GENRE

METHOD   LENGTH

NOTES/QUOTES

BOOK COVER

TITLE

AUTHOR

GENRE

METHOD   LENGTH

NOTES/QUOTES

BOOK COVER

TITLE

AUTHOR

GENRE

METHOD   LENGTH

NOTES/QUOTES

BOOK COVER

TITLE
AUTHOR
GENRE
METHOD   LENGTH
NOTES/QUOTES

BOOK COVER

TITLE
AUTHOR
GENRE
METHOD   LENGTH
NOTES/QUOTES

BOOK COVER

TITLE

AUTHOR

GENRE

METHOD   LENGTH

NOTES/QUOTES

BOOK COVER

TITLE

AUTHOR

GENRE

METHOD   LENGTH

NOTES/QUOTES

BOOK COVER

TITLE

AUTHOR

GENRE

METHOD   LENGTH

NOTES/QUOTES

BOOK COVER

TITLE

AUTHOR

GENRE

METHOD   LENGTH

NOTES/QUOTES

BOOK COVER

TITLE _____

AUTHOR _____

GENRE _____

METHOD _____ LENGTH _____

NOTES/QUOTES

★ ★ ★ ★ ★

BOOK COVER

TITLE _____

AUTHOR _____

GENRE _____

METHOD _____ LENGTH _____

NOTES/QUOTES

★ ★ ★ ★ ★

BOOK COVER

TITLE

AUTHOR

GENRE

METHOD   LENGTH

NOTES/QUOTES

BOOK COVER

TITLE

AUTHOR

GENRE

METHOD   LENGTH

NOTES/QUOTES

BOOK COVER

TITLE _____

AUTHOR _____

GENRE _____

METHOD _____ **LENGTH** _____

NOTES/QUOTES

★ ★ ★ ★ ★

BOOK COVER

TITLE _____

AUTHOR _____

GENRE _____

METHOD _____ **LENGTH** _____

NOTES/QUOTES

★ ★ ★ ★ ★

BOOK COVER

TITLE

AUTHOR

GENRE

METHOD   LENGTH

NOTES/QUOTES

★★★★★

BOOK COVER

TITLE

AUTHOR

GENRE

METHOD   LENGTH

NOTES/QUOTES

★★★★★

BOOK COVER

TITLE

AUTHOR

GENRE

METHOD **LENGTH**

NOTES/QUOTES

BOOK COVER

TITLE

AUTHOR

GENRE

METHOD **LENGTH**

NOTES/QUOTES

BOOK COVER

TITLE

AUTHOR

GENRE

METHOD   LENGTH

NOTES/QUOTES

BOOK COVER

TITLE

AUTHOR

GENRE

METHOD   LENGTH

NOTES/QUOTES

BOOK COVER

TITLE

AUTHOR

GENRE

METHOD LENGTH

NOTES/QUOTES

★★★★★

BOOK COVER

TITLE

AUTHOR

GENRE

METHOD LENGTH

NOTES/QUOTES

★★★★★

BOOK COVER

TITLE

AUTHOR

GENRE

METHOD   LENGTH

NOTES/QUOTES

BOOK COVER

TITLE

AUTHOR

GENRE

METHOD   LENGTH

NOTES/QUOTES

BOOK COVER

TITLE

AUTHOR

GENRE

METHOD　　　　LENGTH

NOTES/QUOTES

BOOK COVER

TITLE

AUTHOR

GENRE

METHOD　　　　LENGTH

NOTES/QUOTES

BOOK COVER

TITLE
AUTHOR
GENRE
METHOD   LENGTH
NOTES/QUOTES

BOOK COVER

TITLE
AUTHOR
GENRE
METHOD   LENGTH
NOTES/QUOTES

BOOK COVER

TITLE

AUTHOR

GENRE

METHOD   LENGTH

NOTES/QUOTES

BOOK COVER

TITLE

AUTHOR

GENRE

METHOD   LENGTH

NOTES/QUOTES

BOOK COVER

TITLE

AUTHOR

GENRE

METHOD   LENGTH

NOTES/QUOTES

★★★★★

BOOK COVER

TITLE

AUTHOR

GENRE

METHOD   LENGTH

NOTES/QUOTES

★★★★★

BOOK COVER

TITLE

AUTHOR

GENRE

METHOD   LENGTH

NOTES/QUOTES

BOOK COVER

TITLE

AUTHOR

GENRE

METHOD   LENGTH

NOTES/QUOTES

BOOK COVER

TITLE
AUTHOR
GENRE
METHOD   LENGTH
NOTES/QUOTES

BOOK COVER

TITLE
AUTHOR
GENRE
METHOD   LENGTH
NOTES/QUOTES

BOOK COVER

TITLE

AUTHOR

GENRE

METHOD   LENGTH

NOTES/QUOTES

BOOK COVER

TITLE

AUTHOR

GENRE

METHOD   LENGTH

NOTES/QUOTES

BOOK COVER

TITLE
AUTHOR
GENRE
METHOD   LENGTH
NOTES/QUOTES

BOOK COVER

TITLE
AUTHOR
GENRE
METHOD   LENGTH
NOTES/QUOTES

BOOK COVER

TITLE

AUTHOR

GENRE

METHOD   LENGTH

NOTES/QUOTES

BOOK COVER

TITLE

AUTHOR

GENRE

METHOD   LENGTH

NOTES/QUOTES

BOOK COVER

TITLE

AUTHOR

GENRE

METHOD   LENGTH

NOTES/QUOTES

BOOK COVER

TITLE

AUTHOR

GENRE

METHOD   LENGTH

NOTES/QUOTES

BOOK COVER

TITLE

AUTHOR

GENRE

METHOD   LENGTH

NOTES/QUOTES

★★★★★

BOOK COVER

TITLE

AUTHOR

GENRE

METHOD   LENGTH

NOTES/QUOTES

★★★★★

BOOK COVER

TITLE

AUTHOR

GENRE

METHOD   LENGTH

NOTES/QUOTES

★★★★★

BOOK COVER

TITLE

AUTHOR

GENRE

METHOD   LENGTH

NOTES/QUOTES

★★★★★

BOOK COVER

TITLE

AUTHOR

GENRE

METHOD   LENGTH

NOTES/QUOTES

BOOK COVER

TITLE

AUTHOR

GENRE

METHOD   LENGTH

NOTES/QUOTES

BOOK COVER

TITLE

AUTHOR

GENRE

METHOD   LENGTH

NOTES/QUOTES

★★★★★

BOOK COVER

TITLE

AUTHOR

GENRE

METHOD   LENGTH

NOTES/QUOTES

★★★★★

BOOK COVER

TITLE

AUTHOR

GENRE

METHOD   LENGTH

NOTES/QUOTES

BOOK COVER

TITLE

AUTHOR

GENRE

METHOD   LENGTH

NOTES/QUOTES

BOOK COVER

TITLE

AUTHOR

GENRE

METHOD   LENGTH

NOTES/QUOTES

BOOK COVER

TITLE

AUTHOR

GENRE

METHOD   LENGTH

NOTES/QUOTES

BOOK COVER

TITLE

AUTHOR

GENRE

METHOD LENGTH

NOTES/QUOTES

BOOK COVER

TITLE

AUTHOR

GENRE

METHOD LENGTH

NOTES/QUOTES

BOOK COVER

TITLE
AUTHOR
GENRE
METHOD   LENGTH
NOTES/QUOTES

BOOK COVER

TITLE
AUTHOR
GENRE
METHOD   LENGTH
NOTES/QUOTES

BOOK COVER

TITLE

AUTHOR

GENRE

METHOD   LENGTH

NOTES/QUOTES

BOOK COVER

TITLE

AUTHOR

GENRE

METHOD   LENGTH

NOTES/QUOTES

BOOK COVER

TITLE

AUTHOR

GENRE

METHOD   LENGTH

NOTES/QUOTES

BOOK COVER

TITLE

AUTHOR

GENRE

METHOD   LENGTH

NOTES/QUOTES

BOOK COVER

TITLE

AUTHOR

GENRE

METHOD   LENGTH

NOTES/QUOTES

BOOK COVER

TITLE

AUTHOR

GENRE

METHOD   LENGTH

NOTES/QUOTES

BOOK COVER

TITLE
AUTHOR
GENRE
METHOD   LENGTH
NOTES/QUOTES

BOOK COVER

TITLE
AUTHOR
GENRE
METHOD   LENGTH
NOTES/QUOTES

BOOK COVER

TITLE
AUTHOR
GENRE
METHOD   LENGTH
NOTES/QUOTES

BOOK COVER

TITLE
AUTHOR
GENRE
METHOD   LENGTH
NOTES/QUOTES

BOOK COVER

TITLE

AUTHOR

GENRE

METHOD   LENGTH

NOTES/QUOTES

★★★★★

BOOK COVER

TITLE

AUTHOR

GENRE

METHOD   LENGTH

NOTES/QUOTES

★★★★★

BOOK COVER

TITLE

AUTHOR

GENRE

METHOD   LENGTH

NOTES/QUOTES

★★★★★

BOOK COVER

TITLE

AUTHOR

GENRE

METHOD   LENGTH

NOTES/QUOTES

★★★★★

BOOK COVER

TITLE

AUTHOR

GENRE

METHOD LENGTH

NOTES/QUOTES

★ ★ ★ ★ ★

BOOK COVER

TITLE

AUTHOR

GENRE

METHOD LENGTH

NOTES/QUOTES

★ ★ ★ ★ ★

BOOK COVER

TITLE
AUTHOR
GENRE
METHOD   LENGTH
NOTES/QUOTES

BOOK COVER

TITLE
AUTHOR
GENRE
METHOD   LENGTH
NOTES/QUOTES

BOOK COVER

TITLE

AUTHOR

GENRE

METHOD　　　LENGTH

NOTES/QUOTES

BOOK COVER

TITLE

AUTHOR

GENRE

METHOD　　　LENGTH

NOTES/QUOTES

BOOK COVER

TITLE

AUTHOR

GENRE

METHOD   LENGTH

NOTES/QUOTES

BOOK COVER

TITLE

AUTHOR

GENRE

METHOD   LENGTH

NOTES/QUOTES

BOOK COVER

TITLE

AUTHOR

GENRE

METHOD   LENGTH

NOTES/QUOTES

BOOK COVER

TITLE

AUTHOR

GENRE

METHOD   LENGTH

NOTES/QUOTES

BOOK COVER

TITLE

AUTHOR

GENRE

METHOD   LENGTH

NOTES/QUOTES

BOOK COVER

TITLE

AUTHOR

GENRE

METHOD   LENGTH

NOTES/QUOTES

BOOK COVER

TITLE
AUTHOR
GENRE
METHOD   LENGTH
NOTES/QUOTES

BOOK COVER

TITLE
AUTHOR
GENRE
METHOD   LENGTH
NOTES/QUOTES

BOOK COVER

TITLE

AUTHOR

GENRE

METHOD　　　　　LENGTH

NOTES/QUOTES

BOOK COVER

TITLE

AUTHOR

GENRE

METHOD　　　　　LENGTH

NOTES/QUOTES

BOOK COVER

TITLE

AUTHOR

GENRE

METHOD   LENGTH

NOTES/QUOTES

BOOK COVER

TITLE

AUTHOR

GENRE

METHOD   LENGTH

NOTES/QUOTES

BOOK COVER

TITLE
AUTHOR
GENRE
METHOD   LENGTH
NOTES/QUOTES

⭐⭐⭐⭐⭐

BOOK COVER

TITLE
AUTHOR
GENRE
METHOD   LENGTH
NOTES/QUOTES

⭐⭐⭐⭐⭐

BOOK COVER

TITLE

AUTHOR

GENRE

METHOD   LENGTH

NOTES/QUOTES

BOOK COVER

TITLE

AUTHOR

GENRE

METHOD   LENGTH

NOTES/QUOTES

BOOK COVER

TITLE
AUTHOR
GENRE
METHOD   LENGTH
NOTES/QUOTES

BOOK COVER

TITLE
AUTHOR
GENRE
METHOD   LENGTH
NOTES/QUOTES

BOOK COVER

TITLE

AUTHOR

GENRE

METHOD   LENGTH

NOTES/QUOTES

BOOK COVER

TITLE

AUTHOR

GENRE

METHOD   LENGTH

NOTES/QUOTES

BOOK COVER

TITLE

AUTHOR

GENRE

METHOD   LENGTH

NOTES/QUOTES

BOOK COVER

TITLE

AUTHOR

GENRE

METHOD   LENGTH

NOTES/QUOTES

BOOK COVER

TITLE

AUTHOR

GENRE

METHOD   LENGTH

NOTES/QUOTES

BOOK COVER

TITLE

AUTHOR

GENRE

METHOD   LENGTH

NOTES/QUOTES

BOOK COVER

TITLE
AUTHOR
GENRE
METHOD   LENGTH
NOTES/QUOTES

BOOK COVER

TITLE
AUTHOR
GENRE
METHOD   LENGTH
NOTES/QUOTES

BOOK COVER

TITLE

AUTHOR

GENRE

METHOD   LENGTH

NOTES/QUOTES

BOOK COVER

TITLE

AUTHOR

GENRE

METHOD   LENGTH

NOTES/QUOTES

BOOK COVER

TITLE

AUTHOR

GENRE

METHOD   LENGTH

NOTES/QUOTES

BOOK COVER

TITLE

AUTHOR

GENRE

METHOD   LENGTH

NOTES/QUOTES

BOOK COVER

TITLE
AUTHOR
GENRE
METHOD   LENGTH
NOTES/QUOTES

BOOK COVER

TITLE
AUTHOR
GENRE
METHOD   LENGTH
NOTES/QUOTES

BOOK COVER

TITLE

AUTHOR

GENRE

METHOD   LENGTH

NOTES/QUOTES

BOOK COVER

TITLE

AUTHOR

GENRE

METHOD   LENGTH

NOTES/QUOTES

BOOK COVER

TITLE
AUTHOR
GENRE
METHOD   LENGTH
NOTES/QUOTES

BOOK COVER

TITLE
AUTHOR
GENRE
METHOD   LENGTH
NOTES/QUOTES

BOOK COVER

TITLE

AUTHOR

GENRE

METHOD   LENGTH

NOTES/QUOTES

BOOK COVER

TITLE

AUTHOR

GENRE

METHOD   LENGTH

NOTES/QUOTES

BOOK COVER

TITLE _____

AUTHOR _____

GENRE _____

METHOD _____ **LENGTH** _____

NOTES/QUOTES

★ ★ ★ ★ ★

BOOK COVER

TITLE _____

AUTHOR _____

GENRE _____

METHOD _____ **LENGTH** _____

NOTES/QUOTES

★ ★ ★ ★ ★

BOOK COVER

TITLE

AUTHOR

GENRE

METHOD   LENGTH

NOTES/QUOTES

BOOK COVER

TITLE

AUTHOR

GENRE

METHOD   LENGTH

NOTES/QUOTES

BOOK COVER

TITLE

AUTHOR

GENRE

METHOD LENGTH

NOTES/QUOTES

BOOK COVER

TITLE

AUTHOR

GENRE

METHOD LENGTH

NOTES/QUOTES

BOOK COVER

TITLE

AUTHOR

GENRE

METHOD   LENGTH

NOTES/QUOTES

BOOK COVER

TITLE

AUTHOR

GENRE

METHOD   LENGTH

NOTES/QUOTES

BOOK COVER

TITLE

AUTHOR

GENRE

METHOD   LENGTH

NOTES/QUOTES

★★★★★

BOOK COVER

TITLE

AUTHOR

GENRE

METHOD   LENGTH

NOTES/QUOTES

★★★★★

BOOK COVER

TITLE

AUTHOR

GENRE

METHOD   LENGTH

NOTES/QUOTES

BOOK COVER

TITLE

AUTHOR

GENRE

METHOD   LENGTH

NOTES/QUOTES

BOOK COVER

TITLE

AUTHOR

GENRE

METHOD   LENGTH

NOTES/QUOTES

★★★★★

BOOK COVER

TITLE

AUTHOR

GENRE

METHOD   LENGTH

NOTES/QUOTES

★★★★★

BOOK COVER

TITLE

AUTHOR

GENRE

METHOD   LENGTH

NOTES/QUOTES

BOOK COVER

TITLE

AUTHOR

GENRE

METHOD   LENGTH

NOTES/QUOTES

BOOK COVER

TITLE
AUTHOR
GENRE
METHOD   LENGTH
NOTES/QUOTES

BOOK COVER

TITLE
AUTHOR
GENRE
METHOD   LENGTH
NOTES/QUOTES

BOOK COVER

TITLE
AUTHOR
GENRE
METHOD   LENGTH
NOTES/QUOTES

BOOK COVER

TITLE
AUTHOR
GENRE
METHOD   LENGTH
NOTES/QUOTES

BOOK COVER

TITLE

AUTHOR

GENRE

METHOD　　　　LENGTH

NOTES/QUOTES

BOOK COVER

TITLE

AUTHOR

GENRE

METHOD　　　　LENGTH

NOTES/QUOTES

BOOK COVER

TITLE

AUTHOR

GENRE

METHOD   LENGTH

NOTES/QUOTES

BOOK COVER

TITLE

AUTHOR

GENRE

METHOD   LENGTH

NOTES/QUOTES

BOOK COVER

TITLE

AUTHOR

GENRE

METHOD LENGTH

NOTES/QUOTES

★★★★★

BOOK COVER

TITLE

AUTHOR

GENRE

METHOD LENGTH

NOTES/QUOTES

★★★★★

BOOK COVER

TITLE

AUTHOR

GENRE

METHOD   LENGTH

NOTES/QUOTES

★★★★★

BOOK COVER

TITLE

AUTHOR

GENRE

METHOD   LENGTH

NOTES/QUOTES

★★★★★

BOOK COVER

TITLE

AUTHOR

GENRE

METHOD LENGTH

NOTES/QUOTES

BOOK COVER

TITLE

AUTHOR

GENRE

METHOD LENGTH

NOTES/QUOTES

BOOK COVER

TITLE
AUTHOR
GENRE
METHOD   LENGTH
NOTES/QUOTES

★★★★★

BOOK COVER

TITLE
AUTHOR
GENRE
METHOD   LENGTH
NOTES/QUOTES

★★★★★

BOOK COVER

TITLE

AUTHOR

GENRE

METHOD   LENGTH

NOTES/QUOTES

BOOK COVER

TITLE

AUTHOR

GENRE

METHOD   LENGTH

NOTES/QUOTES

BOOK COVER

TITLE

AUTHOR

GENRE

METHOD   LENGTH

NOTES/QUOTES

BOOK COVER

TITLE

AUTHOR

GENRE

METHOD   LENGTH

NOTES/QUOTES

BOOK COVER

TITLE _____

AUTHOR _____

GENRE _____

METHOD _____ LENGTH _____

NOTES/QUOTES

★ ★ ★ ★ ★

BOOK COVER

TITLE _____

AUTHOR _____

GENRE _____

METHOD _____ LENGTH _____

NOTES/QUOTES

★ ★ ★ ★ ★

BOOK COVER

TITLE

AUTHOR

GENRE

METHOD   LENGTH

NOTES/QUOTES

BOOK COVER

TITLE

AUTHOR

GENRE

METHOD   LENGTH

NOTES/QUOTES

BOOK COVER

TITLE

AUTHOR

GENRE

METHOD   LENGTH

NOTES/QUOTES

⭐⭐⭐⭐⭐

BOOK COVER

TITLE

AUTHOR

GENRE

METHOD   LENGTH

NOTES/QUOTES

⭐⭐⭐⭐⭐

BOOK COVER

TITLE

AUTHOR

GENRE

METHOD   LENGTH

NOTES/QUOTES

BOOK COVER

TITLE

AUTHOR

GENRE

METHOD   LENGTH

NOTES/QUOTES

BOOK COVER

TITLE

AUTHOR

GENRE

METHOD   LENGTH

NOTES/QUOTES

★★★★★

BOOK COVER

TITLE

AUTHOR

GENRE

METHOD   LENGTH

NOTES/QUOTES

★★★★★

BOOK COVER

TITLE

AUTHOR

GENRE

METHOD   LENGTH

NOTES/QUOTES

★★★★★

BOOK COVER

TITLE

AUTHOR

GENRE

METHOD   LENGTH

NOTES/QUOTES

★★★★★

BOOK COVER

TITLE
AUTHOR
GENRE
METHOD   LENGTH
NOTES/QUOTES

BOOK COVER

TITLE
AUTHOR
GENRE
METHOD   LENGTH
NOTES/QUOTES

BOOK COVER

TITLE
AUTHOR
GENRE
METHOD   LENGTH
NOTES/QUOTES

BOOK COVER

TITLE
AUTHOR
GENRE
METHOD   LENGTH
NOTES/QUOTES

BOOK COVER

TITLE

AUTHOR

GENRE

METHOD　　　　　LENGTH

NOTES/QUOTES

★ ★ ★ ★ ★

BOOK COVER

TITLE

AUTHOR

GENRE

METHOD　　　　　LENGTH

NOTES/QUOTES

★ ★ ★ ★ ★

BOOK COVER

TITLE

AUTHOR

GENRE

METHOD   LENGTH

NOTES/QUOTES

BOOK COVER

TITLE

AUTHOR

GENRE

METHOD   LENGTH

NOTES/QUOTES

BOOK COVER

TITLE

AUTHOR

GENRE

METHOD   LENGTH

NOTES/QUOTES

★ ★ ★ ★ ★

BOOK COVER

TITLE

AUTHOR

GENRE

METHOD   LENGTH

NOTES/QUOTES

★ ★ ★ ★ ★

BOOK COVER

TITLE

AUTHOR

GENRE

METHOD   LENGTH

NOTES/QUOTES

BOOK COVER

TITLE

AUTHOR

GENRE

METHOD   LENGTH

NOTES/QUOTES

BOOK COVER

TITLE

AUTHOR

GENRE

METHOD　　　　LENGTH

NOTES/QUOTES

BOOK COVER

TITLE

AUTHOR

GENRE

METHOD　　　　LENGTH

NOTES/QUOTES

BOOK COVER

TITLE

AUTHOR

GENRE

METHOD   LENGTH

NOTES/QUOTES

BOOK COVER

TITLE

AUTHOR

GENRE

METHOD   LENGTH

NOTES/QUOTES

BOOK COVER

TITLE

AUTHOR

GENRE

METHOD   LENGTH

NOTES/QUOTES

BOOK COVER

TITLE

AUTHOR

GENRE

METHOD   LENGTH

NOTES/QUOTES

BOOK COVER

TITLE

AUTHOR

GENRE

METHOD   LENGTH

NOTES/QUOTES

BOOK COVER

TITLE

AUTHOR

GENRE

METHOD   LENGTH

NOTES/QUOTES

BOOK COVER

TITLE

AUTHOR

GENRE

METHOD   LENGTH

NOTES/QUOTES

★ ★ ★ ★ ★

BOOK COVER

TITLE

AUTHOR

GENRE

METHOD   LENGTH

NOTES/QUOTES

★ ★ ★ ★ ★

BOOK COVER

TITLE

AUTHOR

GENRE

METHOD   LENGTH

NOTES/QUOTES

BOOK COVER

TITLE

AUTHOR

GENRE

METHOD   LENGTH

NOTES/QUOTES

BOOK COVER

TITLE

AUTHOR

GENRE

METHOD　　　　LENGTH

NOTES/QUOTES

BOOK COVER

TITLE

AUTHOR

GENRE

METHOD　　　　LENGTH

NOTES/QUOTES

BOOK COVER

TITLE
AUTHOR
GENRE
METHOD   LENGTH
NOTES/QUOTES

BOOK COVER

TITLE
AUTHOR
GENRE
METHOD   LENGTH
NOTES/QUOTES

BOOK COVER

TITLE
AUTHOR
GENRE
METHOD   LENGTH
NOTES/QUOTES

BOOK COVER

TITLE
AUTHOR
GENRE
METHOD   LENGTH
NOTES/QUOTES

BOOK COVER

TITLE
AUTHOR
GENRE
METHOD   LENGTH
NOTES/QUOTES

★★★★★

BOOK COVER

TITLE
AUTHOR
GENRE
METHOD   LENGTH
NOTES/QUOTES

★★★★★

BOOK COVER

TITLE

AUTHOR

GENRE

METHOD   LENGTH

NOTES/QUOTES

BOOK COVER

TITLE

AUTHOR

GENRE

METHOD   LENGTH

NOTES/QUOTES

BOOK COVER

TITLE

AUTHOR

GENRE

METHOD   LENGTH

NOTES/QUOTES

★★★★★

BOOK COVER

TITLE

AUTHOR

GENRE

METHOD   LENGTH

NOTES/QUOTES

★★★★★

BOOK COVER

TITLE

AUTHOR

GENRE

METHOD   LENGTH

NOTES/QUOTES

★★★★★

BOOK COVER

TITLE

AUTHOR

GENRE

METHOD   LENGTH

NOTES/QUOTES

★★★★★

BOOK COVER

TITLE
AUTHOR
GENRE
METHOD   LENGTH
NOTES/QUOTES

BOOK COVER

TITLE
AUTHOR
GENRE
METHOD   LENGTH
NOTES/QUOTES

BOOK COVER

TITLE
AUTHOR
GENRE
METHOD   LENGTH
NOTES/QUOTES

BOOK COVER

TITLE
AUTHOR
GENRE
METHOD   LENGTH
NOTES/QUOTES

BOOK COVER

TITLE

AUTHOR

GENRE

METHOD   LENGTH

NOTES/QUOTES

BOOK COVER

TITLE

AUTHOR

GENRE

METHOD   LENGTH

NOTES/QUOTES

BOOK COVER

TITLE

AUTHOR

GENRE

METHOD   LENGTH

NOTES/QUOTES

BOOK COVER

TITLE

AUTHOR

GENRE

METHOD   LENGTH

NOTES/QUOTES

BOOK COVER

TITLE

AUTHOR

GENRE

METHOD   LENGTH

NOTES/QUOTES

BOOK COVER

TITLE

AUTHOR

GENRE

METHOD   LENGTH

NOTES/QUOTES

BOOK COVER

TITLE

AUTHOR

GENRE

METHOD   LENGTH

NOTES/QUOTES

BOOK COVER

TITLE

AUTHOR

GENRE

METHOD   LENGTH

NOTES/QUOTES

BOOK COVER

TITLE
AUTHOR
GENRE
METHOD   LENGTH
NOTES/QUOTES

BOOK COVER

TITLE
AUTHOR
GENRE
METHOD   LENGTH
NOTES/QUOTES

BOOK COVER

TITLE

AUTHOR

GENRE

METHOD   LENGTH

NOTES/QUOTES

★★★★★

BOOK COVER

TITLE

AUTHOR

GENRE

METHOD   LENGTH

NOTES/QUOTES

★★★★★

BOOK COVER

TITLE

AUTHOR

GENRE

METHOD   LENGTH

NOTES/QUOTES

BOOK COVER

TITLE

AUTHOR

GENRE

METHOD   LENGTH

NOTES/QUOTES

BOOK COVER

TITLE
AUTHOR
GENRE
METHOD   LENGTH
NOTES/QUOTES

BOOK COVER

TITLE
AUTHOR
GENRE
METHOD   LENGTH
NOTES/QUOTES

BOOK COVER

TITLE

AUTHOR

GENRE

METHOD   LENGTH

NOTES/QUOTES

★ ★ ★ ★ ★

BOOK COVER

TITLE

AUTHOR

GENRE

METHOD   LENGTH

NOTES/QUOTES

★ ★ ★ ★ ★

BOOK COVER

TITLE

AUTHOR

GENRE

METHOD   LENGTH

NOTES/QUOTES

BOOK COVER

TITLE

AUTHOR

GENRE

METHOD   LENGTH

NOTES/QUOTES

BOOK COVER

TITLE

AUTHOR

GENRE

METHOD   LENGTH

NOTES/QUOTES

★★★★★

BOOK COVER

TITLE

AUTHOR

GENRE

METHOD   LENGTH

NOTES/QUOTES

★★★★★

BOOK COVER

TITLE

AUTHOR

GENRE

METHOD   LENGTH

NOTES/QUOTES

BOOK COVER

TITLE

AUTHOR

GENRE

METHOD   LENGTH

NOTES/QUOTES

BOOK COVER

TITLE
AUTHOR
GENRE
METHOD LENGTH
NOTES/QUOTES

BOOK COVER

TITLE
AUTHOR
GENRE
METHOD LENGTH
NOTES/QUOTES

BOOK COVER

TITLE

AUTHOR

GENRE

METHOD   LENGTH

NOTES/QUOTES

BOOK COVER

TITLE

AUTHOR

GENRE

METHOD   LENGTH

NOTES/QUOTES

BOOK COVER

TITLE

AUTHOR

GENRE

METHOD   LENGTH

NOTES/QUOTES

BOOK COVER

TITLE

AUTHOR

GENRE

METHOD   LENGTH

NOTES/QUOTES

BOOK COVER

TITLE
AUTHOR
GENRE
METHOD   LENGTH
NOTES/QUOTES

★★★★★

BOOK COVER

TITLE
AUTHOR
GENRE
METHOD   LENGTH
NOTES/QUOTES

★★★★★

BOOK COVER

TITLE

AUTHOR

GENRE

METHOD   LENGTH

NOTES/QUOTES

★ ★ ★ ★ ★

BOOK COVER

TITLE

AUTHOR

GENRE

METHOD   LENGTH

NOTES/QUOTES

★ ★ ★ ★ ★

BOOK COVER

TITLE
AUTHOR
GENRE
METHOD   LENGTH
NOTES/QUOTES

BOOK COVER

TITLE
AUTHOR
GENRE
METHOD   LENGTH
NOTES/QUOTES

BOOK COVER

TITLE

AUTHOR

GENRE

METHOD   LENGTH

NOTES/QUOTES

BOOK COVER

TITLE

AUTHOR

GENRE

METHOD   LENGTH

NOTES/QUOTES

BOOK COVER

TITLE
AUTHOR
GENRE
METHOD   LENGTH
NOTES/QUOTES

BOOK COVER

TITLE
AUTHOR
GENRE
METHOD   LENGTH
NOTES/QUOTES

BOOK COVER

TITLE
AUTHOR
GENRE
METHOD   LENGTH
NOTES/QUOTES

BOOK COVER

TITLE
AUTHOR
GENRE
METHOD   LENGTH
NOTES/QUOTES

BOOK COVER

TITLE

AUTHOR

GENRE

METHOD **LENGTH**

NOTES/QUOTES

★★★★★

BOOK COVER

TITLE

AUTHOR

GENRE

METHOD **LENGTH**

NOTES/QUOTES

★★★★★

BOOK COVER

TITLE

AUTHOR

GENRE

METHOD   LENGTH

NOTES/QUOTES

BOOK COVER

TITLE

AUTHOR

GENRE

METHOD   LENGTH

NOTES/QUOTES

BOOK COVER

TITLE
AUTHOR
GENRE
METHOD   LENGTH
NOTES/QUOTES

BOOK COVER

TITLE
AUTHOR
GENRE
METHOD   LENGTH
NOTES/QUOTES

BOOK COVER

TITLE

AUTHOR

GENRE

METHOD   LENGTH

NOTES/QUOTES

BOOK COVER

TITLE

AUTHOR

GENRE

METHOD   LENGTH

NOTES/QUOTES

BOOK COVER

TITLE
AUTHOR
GENRE
METHOD   LENGTH
NOTES/QUOTES

BOOK COVER

TITLE
AUTHOR
GENRE
METHOD   LENGTH
NOTES/QUOTES

BOOK COVER

TITLE
AUTHOR
GENRE
METHOD   LENGTH
NOTES/QUOTES

BOOK COVER

TITLE
AUTHOR
GENRE
METHOD   LENGTH
NOTES/QUOTES

BOOK COVER

TITLE

AUTHOR

GENRE

METHOD LENGTH

NOTES/QUOTES

BOOK COVER

TITLE

AUTHOR

GENRE

METHOD LENGTH

NOTES/QUOTES

BOOK COVER

TITLE

AUTHOR

GENRE

METHOD   LENGTH

NOTES/QUOTES

BOOK COVER

TITLE

AUTHOR

GENRE

METHOD   LENGTH

NOTES/QUOTES

BOOK COVER

TITLE

AUTHOR

GENRE

METHOD LENGTH

NOTES/QUOTES

BOOK COVER

TITLE

AUTHOR

GENRE

METHOD LENGTH

NOTES/QUOTES

BOOK COVER

TITLE

AUTHOR

GENRE

METHOD   LENGTH

NOTES/QUOTES

BOOK COVER

TITLE

AUTHOR

GENRE

METHOD   LENGTH

NOTES/QUOTES

BOOK COVER

TITLE

AUTHOR

GENRE

METHOD   LENGTH

NOTES/QUOTES

★★★★★

BOOK COVER

TITLE

AUTHOR

GENRE

METHOD   LENGTH

NOTES/QUOTES

★★★★★

BOOK COVER

TITLE

AUTHOR

GENRE

METHOD   LENGTH

NOTES/QUOTES

BOOK COVER

TITLE

AUTHOR

GENRE

METHOD   LENGTH

NOTES/QUOTES

BOOK COVER

TITLE

AUTHOR

GENRE

METHOD LENGTH

NOTES/QUOTES

★★★★★

BOOK COVER

TITLE

AUTHOR

GENRE

METHOD LENGTH

NOTES/QUOTES

★★★★★

BOOK COVER

TITLE
AUTHOR
GENRE
METHOD   LENGTH
NOTES/QUOTES

BOOK COVER

TITLE
AUTHOR
GENRE
METHOD   LENGTH
NOTES/QUOTES

BOOK COVER

TITLE

AUTHOR

GENRE

METHOD   LENGTH

NOTES/QUOTES

BOOK COVER

TITLE

AUTHOR

GENRE

METHOD   LENGTH

NOTES/QUOTES

BOOK COVER

TITLE

AUTHOR

GENRE

METHOD   LENGTH

NOTES/QUOTES

BOOK COVER

TITLE

AUTHOR

GENRE

METHOD   LENGTH

NOTES/QUOTES

BOOK COVER

TITLE

AUTHOR

GENRE

METHOD   LENGTH

NOTES/QUOTES

BOOK COVER

TITLE

AUTHOR

GENRE

METHOD   LENGTH

NOTES/QUOTES

BOOK COVER

TITLE
AUTHOR
GENRE
METHOD   LENGTH
NOTES/QUOTES

BOOK COVER

TITLE
AUTHOR
GENRE
METHOD   LENGTH
NOTES/QUOTES

BOOK COVER

TITLE

AUTHOR

GENRE

METHOD   LENGTH

NOTES/QUOTES

BOOK COVER

TITLE

AUTHOR

GENRE

METHOD   LENGTH

NOTES/QUOTES

BOOK COVER

TITLE _____

AUTHOR _____

GENRE _____

METHOD _____ LENGTH ____

NOTES/QUOTES

★ ★ ★ ★ ★

BOOK COVER

TITLE _____

AUTHOR _____

GENRE _____

METHOD _____ LENGTH ____

NOTES/QUOTES

★ ★ ★ ★ ★

BOOK COVER

TITLE

AUTHOR

GENRE

METHOD   LENGTH

NOTES/QUOTES

BOOK COVER

TITLE

AUTHOR

GENRE

METHOD   LENGTH

NOTES/QUOTES

BOOK COVER

TITLE _____

AUTHOR _____

GENRE _____

METHOD _____ LENGTH ____

NOTES/QUOTES

★ ★ ★ ★ ★

BOOK COVER

TITLE _____

AUTHOR _____

GENRE _____

METHOD _____ LENGTH ____

NOTES/QUOTES

★ ★ ★ ★ ★

BOOK COVER

TITLE

AUTHOR

GENRE

METHOD LENGTH

NOTES/QUOTES

BOOK COVER

TITLE

AUTHOR

GENRE

METHOD LENGTH

NOTES/QUOTES

BOOK COVER

TITLE
AUTHOR
GENRE
METHOD   LENGTH
NOTES/QUOTES

BOOK COVER

TITLE
AUTHOR
GENRE
METHOD   LENGTH
NOTES/QUOTES

BOOK COVER

TITLE

AUTHOR

GENRE

METHOD　　　　LENGTH

NOTES/QUOTES

BOOK COVER

TITLE

AUTHOR

GENRE

METHOD　　　　LENGTH

NOTES/QUOTES

BOOK COVER

TITLE

AUTHOR

GENRE

METHOD   LENGTH

NOTES/QUOTES

BOOK COVER

TITLE

AUTHOR

GENRE

METHOD   LENGTH

NOTES/QUOTES

BOOK COVER

TITLE

AUTHOR

GENRE

METHOD   LENGTH

NOTES/QUOTES

BOOK COVER

TITLE

AUTHOR

GENRE

METHOD   LENGTH

NOTES/QUOTES

BOOK COVER

TITLE
AUTHOR
GENRE
METHOD   LENGTH
NOTES/QUOTES

★ ★ ★ ★ ★

BOOK COVER

TITLE
AUTHOR
GENRE
METHOD   LENGTH
NOTES/QUOTES

★ ★ ★ ★ ★

BOOK COVER

TITLE

AUTHOR

GENRE

METHOD   LENGTH

NOTES/QUOTES

★★★★★

BOOK COVER

TITLE

AUTHOR

GENRE

METHOD   LENGTH

NOTES/QUOTES

★★★★★

BOOK COVER

TITLE
AUTHOR
GENRE
METHOD   LENGTH
NOTES/QUOTES

★ ★ ★ ★ ★

BOOK COVER

TITLE
AUTHOR
GENRE
METHOD   LENGTH
NOTES/QUOTES

★ ★ ★ ★ ★

BOOK COVER

TITLE
AUTHOR
GENRE
METHOD   LENGTH
NOTES/QUOTES

BOOK COVER

TITLE
AUTHOR
GENRE
METHOD   LENGTH
NOTES/QUOTES

BOOK COVER

TITLE
AUTHOR
GENRE
METHOD   LENGTH
NOTES/QUOTES

★★★★★

BOOK COVER

TITLE
AUTHOR
GENRE
METHOD   LENGTH
NOTES/QUOTES

★★★★★

BOOK COVER

TITLE _____

AUTHOR _____

GENRE _____

METHOD _____ LENGTH _____

NOTES/QUOTES

★★★★★

BOOK COVER

TITLE _____

AUTHOR _____

GENRE _____

METHOD _____ LENGTH _____

NOTES/QUOTES

★★★★★

BOOK COVER

TITLE

AUTHOR

GENRE

METHOD   LENGTH

NOTES/QUOTES

★★★★★

BOOK COVER

TITLE

AUTHOR

GENRE

METHOD   LENGTH

NOTES/QUOTES

★★★★★

BOOK COVER

TITLE

AUTHOR

GENRE

METHOD   LENGTH

NOTES/QUOTES

BOOK COVER

TITLE

AUTHOR

GENRE

METHOD   LENGTH

NOTES/QUOTES

BOOK COVER

TITLE
AUTHOR
GENRE
METHOD   LENGTH
NOTES/QUOTES

★ ★ ★ ★ ★

BOOK COVER

TITLE
AUTHOR
GENRE
METHOD   LENGTH
NOTES/QUOTES

★ ★ ★ ★ ★

BOOK COVER

TITLE

AUTHOR

GENRE

METHOD   LENGTH

NOTES/QUOTES

BOOK COVER

TITLE

AUTHOR

GENRE

METHOD   LENGTH

NOTES/QUOTES

BOOK COVER

TITLE

AUTHOR

GENRE

METHOD   LENGTH

NOTES/QUOTES

BOOK COVER

TITLE

AUTHOR

GENRE

METHOD   LENGTH

NOTES/QUOTES

BOOK COVER

TITLE
AUTHOR
GENRE
METHOD   LENGTH
NOTES/QUOTES

★★★★★

BOOK COVER

TITLE
AUTHOR
GENRE
METHOD   LENGTH
NOTES/QUOTES

★★★★★

BOOK COVER

TITLE
AUTHOR
GENRE
METHOD   LENGTH
NOTES/QUOTES

BOOK COVER

TITLE
AUTHOR
GENRE
METHOD   LENGTH
NOTES/QUOTES

BOOK COVER

TITLE

AUTHOR

GENRE

METHOD   LENGTH

NOTES/QUOTES

BOOK COVER

TITLE

AUTHOR

GENRE

METHOD   LENGTH

NOTES/QUOTES

BOOK COVER

TITLE
AUTHOR
GENRE
METHOD   LENGTH
NOTES/QUOTES

BOOK COVER

TITLE
AUTHOR
GENRE
METHOD   LENGTH
NOTES/QUOTES

BOOK COVER

TITLE

AUTHOR

GENRE

METHOD   LENGTH

NOTES/QUOTES

BOOK COVER

TITLE

AUTHOR

GENRE

METHOD   LENGTH

NOTES/QUOTES

BOOK COVER

TITLE
AUTHOR
GENRE
METHOD   LENGTH
NOTES/QUOTES

BOOK COVER

TITLE
AUTHOR
GENRE
METHOD   LENGTH
NOTES/QUOTES

BOOK COVER

TITLE

AUTHOR

GENRE

METHOD   LENGTH

NOTES/QUOTES

BOOK COVER

TITLE

AUTHOR

GENRE

METHOD   LENGTH

NOTES/QUOTES

BOOK COVER

TITLE
AUTHOR
GENRE
METHOD   LENGTH
NOTES/QUOTES

BOOK COVER

TITLE
AUTHOR
GENRE
METHOD   LENGTH
NOTES/QUOTES

BOOK COVER

TITLE

AUTHOR

GENRE

METHOD LENGTH

NOTES/QUOTES

BOOK COVER

TITLE

AUTHOR

GENRE

METHOD LENGTH

NOTES/QUOTES

BOOK COVER

TITLE
AUTHOR
GENRE
METHOD   LENGTH
NOTES/QUOTES

★★★★★

BOOK COVER

TITLE
AUTHOR
GENRE
METHOD   LENGTH
NOTES/QUOTES

★★★★★

BOOK COVER

TITLE

AUTHOR

GENRE

METHOD   LENGTH

NOTES/QUOTES

BOOK COVER

TITLE

AUTHOR

GENRE

METHOD   LENGTH

NOTES/QUOTES

BOOK COVER

TITLE

AUTHOR

GENRE

METHOD   LENGTH

NOTES/QUOTES

BOOK COVER

TITLE

AUTHOR

GENRE

METHOD   LENGTH

NOTES/QUOTES

BOOK COVER

TITLE

AUTHOR

GENRE

METHOD   LENGTH

NOTES/QUOTES

★★★★★

BOOK COVER

TITLE

AUTHOR

GENRE

METHOD   LENGTH

NOTES/QUOTES

★★★★★

BOOK COVER

TITLE

AUTHOR

GENRE

METHOD   LENGTH

NOTES/QUOTES

★★★★★

BOOK COVER

TITLE

AUTHOR

GENRE

METHOD   LENGTH

NOTES/QUOTES

★★★★★

BOOK COVER

TITLE

AUTHOR

GENRE

METHOD   LENGTH

NOTES/QUOTES

★★★★★

BOOK COVER

TITLE

AUTHOR

GENRE

METHOD   LENGTH

NOTES/QUOTES

★★★★★

BOOK COVER

TITLE

AUTHOR

GENRE

METHOD   LENGTH

NOTES/QUOTES

BOOK COVER

TITLE

AUTHOR

GENRE

METHOD   LENGTH

NOTES/QUOTES

BOOK COVER

TITLE

AUTHOR

GENRE

METHOD   LENGTH

NOTES/QUOTES

BOOK COVER

TITLE

AUTHOR

GENRE

METHOD   LENGTH

NOTES/QUOTES

BOOK COVER

TITLE

AUTHOR

GENRE

METHOD   LENGTH

NOTES/QUOTES

★ ★ ★ ★ ★

BOOK COVER

TITLE

AUTHOR

GENRE

METHOD   LENGTH

NOTES/QUOTES

★ ★ ★ ★ ★

BOOK COVER

TITLE

AUTHOR

GENRE

METHOD   LENGTH

NOTES/QUOTES

★ ★ ★ ★ ★

BOOK COVER

TITLE

AUTHOR

GENRE

METHOD   LENGTH

NOTES/QUOTES

★ ★ ★ ★ ★

BOOK COVER

TITLE

AUTHOR

GENRE

METHOD　　　　　LENGTH

NOTES/QUOTES

BOOK COVER

TITLE

AUTHOR

GENRE

METHOD　　　　　LENGTH

NOTES/QUOTES

BOOK COVER

TITLE

AUTHOR

GENRE

METHOD   LENGTH

NOTES/QUOTES

★★★★★

BOOK COVER

TITLE

AUTHOR

GENRE

METHOD   LENGTH

NOTES/QUOTES

★★★★★

BOOK COVER

TITLE

AUTHOR

GENRE

METHOD   LENGTH

NOTES/QUOTES

BOOK COVER

TITLE

AUTHOR

GENRE

METHOD   LENGTH

NOTES/QUOTES

BOOK COVER

TITLE

AUTHOR

GENRE

METHOD   LENGTH

NOTES/QUOTES

BOOK COVER

TITLE

AUTHOR

GENRE

METHOD   LENGTH

NOTES/QUOTES

BOOK COVER

TITLE

AUTHOR

GENRE

METHOD   LENGTH

NOTES/QUOTES

BOOK COVER

TITLE

AUTHOR

GENRE

METHOD   LENGTH

NOTES/QUOTES

BOOK COVER

TITLE
AUTHOR
GENRE
METHOD   LENGTH
NOTES/QUOTES

★★★★★

BOOK COVER

TITLE
AUTHOR
GENRE
METHOD   LENGTH
NOTES/QUOTES

★★★★★

BOOK COVER

TITLE
AUTHOR
GENRE
METHOD   LENGTH
NOTES/QUOTES

★★★★★

BOOK COVER

TITLE
AUTHOR
GENRE
METHOD   LENGTH
NOTES/QUOTES

★★★★★

BOOK COVER

TITLE

AUTHOR

GENRE

METHOD   LENGTH

NOTES/QUOTES

BOOK COVER

TITLE

AUTHOR

GENRE

METHOD   LENGTH

NOTES/QUOTES

BOOK COVER

TITLE

AUTHOR

GENRE

METHOD   LENGTH

NOTES/QUOTES

BOOK COVER

TITLE

AUTHOR

GENRE

METHOD   LENGTH

NOTES/QUOTES

BOOK COVER

TITLE
AUTHOR
GENRE
METHOD   LENGTH
NOTES/QUOTES

★★★★★

BOOK COVER

TITLE
AUTHOR
GENRE
METHOD   LENGTH
NOTES/QUOTES

★★★★★

BOOK COVER

TITLE
AUTHOR
GENRE
METHOD   LENGTH
NOTES/QUOTES

BOOK COVER

TITLE
AUTHOR
GENRE
METHOD   LENGTH
NOTES/QUOTES

BOOK COVER

TITLE	
AUTHOR	
GENRE	
METHOD	LENGTH
NOTES/QUOTES	

★ ★ ★ ★ ★

BOOK COVER

TITLE	
AUTHOR	
GENRE	
METHOD	LENGTH
NOTES/QUOTES	

★ ★ ★ ★ ★

BOOK COVER

TITLE
AUTHOR
GENRE
METHOD   LENGTH
NOTES/QUOTES

BOOK COVER

TITLE
AUTHOR
GENRE
METHOD   LENGTH
NOTES/QUOTES

BOOK COVER

TITLE

AUTHOR

GENRE

METHOD   LENGTH

NOTES/QUOTES

BOOK COVER

TITLE

AUTHOR

GENRE

METHOD   LENGTH

NOTES/QUOTES

BOOK COVER

TITLE

AUTHOR

GENRE

METHOD   LENGTH

NOTES/QUOTES

★★★★★

BOOK COVER

TITLE

AUTHOR

GENRE

METHOD   LENGTH

NOTES/QUOTES

★★★★★

BOOK COVER

TITLE

AUTHOR

GENRE

METHOD   LENGTH

NOTES/QUOTES

BOOK COVER

TITLE

AUTHOR

GENRE

METHOD   LENGTH

NOTES/QUOTES

BOOK COVER

TITLE

AUTHOR

GENRE

METHOD   LENGTH

NOTES/QUOTES

BOOK COVER

TITLE

AUTHOR

GENRE

METHOD   LENGTH

NOTES/QUOTES

BOOK COVER

TITLE _____

AUTHOR _____

GENRE _____

METHOD _____ **LENGTH** _____

NOTES/QUOTES

⭐⭐⭐⭐⭐

BOOK COVER

TITLE _____

AUTHOR _____

GENRE _____

METHOD _____ **LENGTH** _____

NOTES/QUOTES

⭐⭐⭐⭐⭐

BOOK COVER

TITLE
AUTHOR
GENRE
METHOD   LENGTH
NOTES/QUOTES

BOOK COVER

TITLE
AUTHOR
GENRE
METHOD   LENGTH
NOTES/QUOTES

BOOK COVER

TITLE
AUTHOR
GENRE
METHOD   LENGTH
NOTES/QUOTES

BOOK COVER

TITLE
AUTHOR
GENRE
METHOD   LENGTH
NOTES/QUOTES

BOOK COVER

TITLE
AUTHOR
GENRE
METHOD   LENGTH
NOTES/QUOTES

★ ★ ★ ★ ★

BOOK COVER

TITLE
AUTHOR
GENRE
METHOD   LENGTH
NOTES/QUOTES

★ ★ ★ ★ ★

BOOK COVER

TITLE
AUTHOR
GENRE
METHOD   LENGTH
NOTES/QUOTES

BOOK COVER

TITLE
AUTHOR
GENRE
METHOD   LENGTH
NOTES/QUOTES

BOOK COVER

TITLE

AUTHOR

GENRE

METHOD   LENGTH

NOTES/QUOTES

★★★★★

BOOK COVER

TITLE

AUTHOR

GENRE

METHOD   LENGTH

NOTES/QUOTES

★★★★★

BOOK COVER

TITLE
AUTHOR
GENRE
METHOD   LENGTH
NOTES/QUOTES

BOOK COVER

TITLE
AUTHOR
GENRE
METHOD   LENGTH
NOTES/QUOTES

BOOK COVER

TITLE
AUTHOR
GENRE
METHOD   LENGTH
NOTES/QUOTES

★ ★ ★ ★ ★

BOOK COVER

TITLE
AUTHOR
GENRE
METHOD   LENGTH
NOTES/QUOTES

★ ★ ★ ★ ★

BOOK COVER

TITLE
AUTHOR
GENRE
METHOD   LENGTH
NOTES/QUOTES

BOOK COVER

TITLE
AUTHOR
GENRE
METHOD   LENGTH
NOTES/QUOTES

BOOK COVER

TITLE

AUTHOR

GENRE

METHOD   LENGTH

NOTES/QUOTES

★ ★ ★ ★ ★

BOOK COVER

TITLE

AUTHOR

GENRE

METHOD   LENGTH

NOTES/QUOTES

★ ★ ★ ★ ★

BOOK COVER

TITLE
AUTHOR
GENRE
METHOD   LENGTH
NOTES/QUOTES

BOOK COVER

TITLE
AUTHOR
GENRE
METHOD   LENGTH
NOTES/QUOTES

BOOK COVER

TITLE
AUTHOR
GENRE
METHOD   LENGTH
NOTES/QUOTES

★★★★★

BOOK COVER

TITLE
AUTHOR
GENRE
METHOD   LENGTH
NOTES/QUOTES

★★★★★

BOOK COVER

TITLE

AUTHOR

GENRE

METHOD   LENGTH

NOTES/QUOTES

BOOK COVER

TITLE

AUTHOR

GENRE

METHOD   LENGTH

NOTES/QUOTES

BOOK COVER

TITLE
AUTHOR
GENRE
METHOD   LENGTH
NOTES/QUOTES

★★★★★

BOOK COVER

TITLE
AUTHOR
GENRE
METHOD   LENGTH
NOTES/QUOTES

★★★★★

BOOK COVER

TITLE

AUTHOR

GENRE

METHOD   LENGTH

NOTES/QUOTES

BOOK COVER

TITLE

AUTHOR

GENRE

METHOD   LENGTH

NOTES/QUOTES

BOOK COVER

TITLE

AUTHOR

GENRE

METHOD   LENGTH

NOTES/QUOTES

★★★★★

BOOK COVER

TITLE

AUTHOR

GENRE

METHOD   LENGTH

NOTES/QUOTES

★★★★★

BOOK COVER

TITLE
AUTHOR
GENRE
METHOD   LENGTH
NOTES/QUOTES

BOOK COVER

TITLE
AUTHOR
GENRE
METHOD   LENGTH
NOTES/QUOTES

BOOK COVER

TITLE
AUTHOR
GENRE
METHOD   LENGTH
NOTES/QUOTES

BOOK COVER

TITLE
AUTHOR
GENRE
METHOD   LENGTH
NOTES/QUOTES

BOOK COVER

TITLE

AUTHOR

GENRE

METHOD   LENGTH

NOTES/QUOTES

★ ★ ★ ★ ★

BOOK COVER

TITLE

AUTHOR

GENRE

METHOD   LENGTH

NOTES/QUOTES

★ ★ ★ ★ ★

BOOK COVER

TITLE

AUTHOR

GENRE

METHOD   LENGTH

NOTES/QUOTES

BOOK COVER

TITLE

AUTHOR

GENRE

METHOD   LENGTH

NOTES/QUOTES

BOOK COVER

TITLE
AUTHOR
GENRE
METHOD   LENGTH
NOTES/QUOTES

BOOK COVER

TITLE
AUTHOR
GENRE
METHOD   LENGTH
NOTES/QUOTES

BOOK COVER

TITLE
AUTHOR
GENRE
METHOD   LENGTH
NOTES/QUOTES

BOOK COVER

TITLE
AUTHOR
GENRE
METHOD   LENGTH
NOTES/QUOTES

BOOK COVER

TITLE

AUTHOR

GENRE

METHOD   LENGTH

NOTES/QUOTES

BOOK COVER

TITLE

AUTHOR

GENRE

METHOD   LENGTH

NOTES/QUOTES

BOOK COVER

TITLE

AUTHOR

GENRE

METHOD   LENGTH

NOTES/QUOTES

BOOK COVER

TITLE

AUTHOR

GENRE

METHOD   LENGTH

NOTES/QUOTES

BOOK COVER

TITLE
AUTHOR
GENRE
METHOD   LENGTH
NOTES/QUOTES

BOOK COVER

TITLE
AUTHOR
GENRE
METHOD   LENGTH
NOTES/QUOTES

BOOK COVER

TITLE
AUTHOR
GENRE
METHOD   LENGTH
NOTES/QUOTES

BOOK COVER

TITLE
AUTHOR
GENRE
METHOD   LENGTH
NOTES/QUOTES

BOOK COVER

TITLE

AUTHOR

GENRE

METHOD LENGTH

NOTES/QUOTES

★★★★★

BOOK COVER

TITLE

AUTHOR

GENRE

METHOD LENGTH

NOTES/QUOTES

★★★★★

BOOK COVER

TITLE

AUTHOR

GENRE

METHOD LENGTH

NOTES/QUOTES

BOOK COVER

TITLE

AUTHOR

GENRE

METHOD LENGTH

NOTES/QUOTES

BOOK COVER

TITLE
AUTHOR
GENRE
METHOD   LENGTH
NOTES/QUOTES

⭐⭐⭐⭐⭐

BOOK COVER

TITLE
AUTHOR
GENRE
METHOD   LENGTH
NOTES/QUOTES

⭐⭐⭐⭐⭐

BOOK COVER

TITLE
AUTHOR
GENRE
METHOD   LENGTH
NOTES/QUOTES

BOOK COVER

TITLE
AUTHOR
GENRE
METHOD   LENGTH
NOTES/QUOTES

BOOK COVER

TITLE _____

AUTHOR _____

GENRE _____

METHOD _____ **LENGTH** _____

NOTES/QUOTES

BOOK COVER

TITLE _____

AUTHOR _____

GENRE _____

METHOD _____ **LENGTH** _____

NOTES/QUOTES

BOOK COVER

TITLE

AUTHOR

GENRE

METHOD   LENGTH

NOTES/QUOTES

★ ★ ★ ★ ★

BOOK COVER

TITLE

AUTHOR

GENRE

METHOD   LENGTH

NOTES/QUOTES

★ ★ ★ ★ ★

BOOK COVER

TITLE

AUTHOR

GENRE

METHOD   LENGTH

NOTES/QUOTES

★★★★★

BOOK COVER

TITLE

AUTHOR

GENRE

METHOD   LENGTH

NOTES/QUOTES

★★★★★

BOOK COVER

TITLE
AUTHOR
GENRE
METHOD   LENGTH
NOTES/QUOTES

BOOK COVER

TITLE
AUTHOR
GENRE
METHOD   LENGTH
NOTES/QUOTES

BOOK COVER

TITLE
AUTHOR
GENRE
METHOD   LENGTH
NOTES/QUOTES

BOOK COVER

TITLE
AUTHOR
GENRE
METHOD   LENGTH
NOTES/QUOTES

BOOK COVER

TITLE
AUTHOR
GENRE
METHOD   LENGTH
NOTES/QUOTES

BOOK COVER

TITLE
AUTHOR
GENRE
METHOD   LENGTH
NOTES/QUOTES

BOOK COVER

TITLE
AUTHOR
GENRE
METHOD   LENGTH
NOTES/QUOTES

BOOK COVER

TITLE
AUTHOR
GENRE
METHOD   LENGTH
NOTES/QUOTES

BOOK COVER

TITLE

AUTHOR

GENRE

METHOD   LENGTH

NOTES/QUOTES

BOOK COVER

TITLE

AUTHOR

GENRE

METHOD   LENGTH

NOTES/QUOTES

BOOK COVER

TITLE
AUTHOR
GENRE
METHOD   LENGTH
NOTES/QUOTES

BOOK COVER

TITLE
AUTHOR
GENRE
METHOD   LENGTH
NOTES/QUOTES

BOOK COVER

TITLE
AUTHOR
GENRE
METHOD LENGTH
NOTES/QUOTES

★★★★★

BOOK COVER

TITLE
AUTHOR
GENRE
METHOD LENGTH
NOTES/QUOTES

★★★★★

BOOK COVER

TITLE
AUTHOR
GENRE
METHOD   LENGTH
NOTES/QUOTES

BOOK COVER

TITLE
AUTHOR
GENRE
METHOD   LENGTH
NOTES/QUOTES

BOOK COVER

TITLE
AUTHOR
GENRE
METHOD   LENGTH
NOTES/QUOTES

BOOK COVER

TITLE
AUTHOR
GENRE
METHOD   LENGTH
NOTES/QUOTES

BOOK COVER

TITLE

AUTHOR

GENRE

METHOD   LENGTH

NOTES/QUOTES

BOOK COVER

TITLE

AUTHOR

GENRE

METHOD   LENGTH

NOTES/QUOTES

BOOK COVER

TITLE
AUTHOR
GENRE
METHOD   LENGTH
NOTES/QUOTES

BOOK COVER

TITLE
AUTHOR
GENRE
METHOD   LENGTH
NOTES/QUOTES

BOOK COVER

TITLE
AUTHOR
GENRE
METHOD   LENGTH
NOTES/QUOTES

BOOK COVER

TITLE
AUTHOR
GENRE
METHOD   LENGTH
NOTES/QUOTES

BOOK COVER

TITLE

AUTHOR

GENRE

METHOD   LENGTH

NOTES/QUOTES

BOOK COVER

TITLE

AUTHOR

GENRE

METHOD   LENGTH

NOTES/QUOTES

BOOK COVER

TITLE

AUTHOR

GENRE

METHOD   LENGTH

NOTES/QUOTES

★★★★★

BOOK COVER

TITLE

AUTHOR

GENRE

METHOD   LENGTH

NOTES/QUOTES

★★★★★

BOOK COVER

TITLE

AUTHOR

GENRE

METHOD   LENGTH

NOTES/QUOTES

BOOK COVER

TITLE

AUTHOR

GENRE

METHOD   LENGTH

NOTES/QUOTES

BOOK COVER

TITLE

AUTHOR

GENRE

METHOD   LENGTH

NOTES/QUOTES

★ ★ ★ ★ ★

BOOK COVER

TITLE

AUTHOR

GENRE

METHOD   LENGTH

NOTES/QUOTES

★ ★ ★ ★ ★

BOOK COVER

TITLE

AUTHOR

GENRE

METHOD   LENGTH

NOTES/QUOTES

⭐⭐⭐⭐⭐

BOOK COVER

TITLE

AUTHOR

GENRE

METHOD   LENGTH

NOTES/QUOTES

⭐⭐⭐⭐⭐

BOOK COVER

TITLE
AUTHOR
GENRE
METHOD   LENGTH
NOTES/QUOTES

BOOK COVER

TITLE
AUTHOR
GENRE
METHOD   LENGTH
NOTES/QUOTES

BOOK COVER

TITLE
AUTHOR
GENRE
METHOD   LENGTH
NOTES/QUOTES

★★★★★

BOOK COVER

TITLE
AUTHOR
GENRE
METHOD   LENGTH
NOTES/QUOTES

★★★★★

BOOK COVER

TITLE
AUTHOR
GENRE
METHOD   LENGTH
NOTES/QUOTES

BOOK COVER

TITLE
AUTHOR
GENRE
METHOD   LENGTH
NOTES/QUOTES

BOOK COVER

TITLE
AUTHOR
GENRE
METHOD   LENGTH
NOTES/QUOTES

BOOK COVER

TITLE
AUTHOR
GENRE
METHOD   LENGTH
NOTES/QUOTES

BOOK COVER

TITLE
AUTHOR
GENRE
METHOD   LENGTH
NOTES/QUOTES

★★★★★

BOOK COVER

TITLE
AUTHOR
GENRE
METHOD   LENGTH
NOTES/QUOTES

★★★★★

BOOK COVER

TITLE

AUTHOR

GENRE

METHOD   LENGTH

NOTES/QUOTES

BOOK COVER

TITLE

AUTHOR

GENRE

METHOD   LENGTH

NOTES/QUOTES

BOOK COVER

TITLE
AUTHOR
GENRE
METHOD   LENGTH
NOTES/QUOTES

★★★★★

BOOK COVER

TITLE
AUTHOR
GENRE
METHOD   LENGTH
NOTES/QUOTES

★★★★★

BOOK COVER

TITLE
AUTHOR
GENRE
METHOD   LENGTH
NOTES/QUOTES

★ ★ ★ ★ ★

BOOK COVER

TITLE
AUTHOR
GENRE
METHOD   LENGTH
NOTES/QUOTES

★ ★ ★ ★ ★

BOOK COVER

TITLE

AUTHOR

GENRE

METHOD   LENGTH

NOTES/QUOTES

BOOK COVER

TITLE

AUTHOR

GENRE

METHOD   LENGTH

NOTES/QUOTES

BOOK COVER

TITLE
AUTHOR
GENRE
METHOD   LENGTH
NOTES/QUOTES

★ ★ ★ ★ ★

BOOK COVER

TITLE
AUTHOR
GENRE
METHOD   LENGTH
NOTES/QUOTES

★ ★ ★ ★ ★

BOOK COVER

TITLE

AUTHOR

GENRE

METHOD　　　　LENGTH

NOTES/QUOTES

★★★★★

BOOK COVER

TITLE

AUTHOR

GENRE

METHOD　　　　LENGTH

NOTES/QUOTES

★★★★★

BOOK COVER

TITLE

AUTHOR

GENRE

METHOD   LENGTH

NOTES/QUOTES

★★★★★

BOOK COVER

TITLE

AUTHOR

GENRE

METHOD   LENGTH

NOTES/QUOTES

★★★★★

BOOK COVER

TITLE

AUTHOR

GENRE

METHOD   LENGTH

NOTES/QUOTES

BOOK COVER

TITLE

AUTHOR

GENRE

METHOD   LENGTH

NOTES/QUOTES

BOOK COVER

TITLE
AUTHOR
GENRE
METHOD   LENGTH
NOTES/QUOTES

BOOK COVER

TITLE
AUTHOR
GENRE
METHOD   LENGTH
NOTES/QUOTES

BOOK COVER

TITLE
AUTHOR
GENRE
METHOD   LENGTH
NOTES/QUOTES

BOOK COVER

TITLE
AUTHOR
GENRE
METHOD   LENGTH
NOTES/QUOTES

BOOK COVER

TITLE
AUTHOR
GENRE
METHOD   LENGTH
NOTES/QUOTES

BOOK COVER

TITLE
AUTHOR
GENRE
METHOD   LENGTH
NOTES/QUOTES

BOOK COVER

TITLE

AUTHOR

GENRE

METHOD   LENGTH

NOTES/QUOTES

BOOK COVER

TITLE

AUTHOR

GENRE

METHOD   LENGTH

NOTES/QUOTES

BOOK COVER

TITLE
AUTHOR
GENRE
METHOD			LENGTH
NOTES/QUOTES

BOOK COVER

TITLE
AUTHOR
GENRE
METHOD			LENGTH
NOTES/QUOTES

BOOK COVER

TITLE

AUTHOR

GENRE

METHOD   LENGTH

NOTES/QUOTES

BOOK COVER

TITLE

AUTHOR

GENRE

METHOD   LENGTH

NOTES/QUOTES

BOOK COVER

TITLE

AUTHOR

GENRE

METHOD   LENGTH

NOTES/QUOTES

★ ★ ★ ★ ★

BOOK COVER

TITLE

AUTHOR

GENRE

METHOD   LENGTH

NOTES/QUOTES

★ ★ ★ ★ ★

BOOK COVER

TITLE
AUTHOR
GENRE
METHOD   LENGTH
NOTES/QUOTES

BOOK COVER

TITLE
AUTHOR
GENRE
METHOD   LENGTH
NOTES/QUOTES

BOOK COVER

TITLE

AUTHOR

GENRE

METHOD LENGTH

NOTES/QUOTES

BOOK COVER

TITLE

AUTHOR

GENRE

METHOD LENGTH

NOTES/QUOTES

BOOK COVER

TITLE

AUTHOR

GENRE

METHOD   LENGTH

NOTES/QUOTES

BOOK COVER

TITLE

AUTHOR

GENRE

METHOD   LENGTH

NOTES/QUOTES

BOOK COVER

TITLE
AUTHOR
GENRE
METHOD   LENGTH
NOTES/QUOTES

BOOK COVER

TITLE
AUTHOR
GENRE
METHOD   LENGTH
NOTES/QUOTES

BOOK COVER

TITLE
AUTHOR
GENRE
METHOD   LENGTH
NOTES/QUOTES

BOOK COVER

TITLE
AUTHOR
GENRE
METHOD   LENGTH
NOTES/QUOTES

BOOK COVER

TITLE
AUTHOR
GENRE
METHOD   LENGTH
NOTES/QUOTES

BOOK COVER

TITLE
AUTHOR
GENRE
METHOD   LENGTH
NOTES/QUOTES

BOOK COVER

TITLE
AUTHOR
GENRE
METHOD   LENGTH
NOTES/QUOTES

BOOK COVER

TITLE
AUTHOR
GENRE
METHOD   LENGTH
NOTES/QUOTES

BOOK COVER

TITLE
AUTHOR
GENRE
METHOD   LENGTH
NOTES/QUOTES

BOOK COVER

TITLE
AUTHOR
GENRE
METHOD   LENGTH
NOTES/QUOTES

BOOK COVER

TITLE

AUTHOR

GENRE

METHOD　　　　　LENGTH

NOTES/QUOTES

★★★★★

BOOK COVER

TITLE

AUTHOR

GENRE

METHOD　　　　　LENGTH

NOTES/QUOTES

★★★★★

BOOK COVER

TITLE
AUTHOR
GENRE
METHOD   LENGTH
NOTES/QUOTES

★ ★ ★ ★ ★

BOOK COVER

TITLE
AUTHOR
GENRE
METHOD   LENGTH
NOTES/QUOTES

★ ★ ★ ★ ★

BOOK COVER

TITLE
AUTHOR
GENRE
METHOD   LENGTH
NOTES/QUOTES

★★★★★

BOOK COVER

TITLE
AUTHOR
GENRE
METHOD   LENGTH
NOTES/QUOTES

★★★★★

BOOK COVER

TITLE

AUTHOR

GENRE

METHOD   LENGTH

NOTES/QUOTES

★★★★★

BOOK COVER

TITLE

AUTHOR

GENRE

METHOD   LENGTH

NOTES/QUOTES

★★★★★

BOOK COVER

TITLE
AUTHOR
GENRE
METHOD   LENGTH
NOTES/QUOTES

BOOK COVER

TITLE
AUTHOR
GENRE
METHOD   LENGTH
NOTES/QUOTES

BOOK COVER

TITLE
AUTHOR
GENRE
METHOD   LENGTH
NOTES/QUOTES

BOOK COVER

TITLE
AUTHOR
GENRE
METHOD   LENGTH
NOTES/QUOTES

BOOK COVER

TITLE

AUTHOR

GENRE

METHOD   LENGTH

NOTES/QUOTES

BOOK COVER

TITLE

AUTHOR

GENRE

METHOD   LENGTH

NOTES/QUOTES

BOOK COVER

TITLE
AUTHOR
GENRE
METHOD   LENGTH
NOTES/QUOTES

★★★★★

BOOK COVER

TITLE
AUTHOR
GENRE
METHOD   LENGTH
NOTES/QUOTES

★★★★★

BOOK COVER

TITLE
AUTHOR
GENRE
METHOD   LENGTH
NOTES/QUOTES

BOOK COVER

TITLE
AUTHOR
GENRE
METHOD   LENGTH
NOTES/QUOTES

BOOK COVER

TITLE

AUTHOR

GENRE

METHOD   LENGTH

NOTES/QUOTES

BOOK COVER

TITLE

AUTHOR

GENRE

METHOD   LENGTH

NOTES/QUOTES

BOOK COVER

TITLE
AUTHOR
GENRE
METHOD   LENGTH
NOTES/QUOTES

BOOK COVER

TITLE
AUTHOR
GENRE
METHOD   LENGTH
NOTES/QUOTES

BOOK COVER

TITLE
AUTHOR
GENRE
METHOD   LENGTH
NOTES/QUOTES

BOOK COVER

TITLE
AUTHOR
GENRE
METHOD   LENGTH
NOTES/QUOTES

BOOK COVER

TITLE
AUTHOR
GENRE
METHOD   LENGTH
NOTES/QUOTES

★★★★★

BOOK COVER

TITLE
AUTHOR
GENRE
METHOD   LENGTH
NOTES/QUOTES

★★★★★

BOOK COVER

TITLE

AUTHOR

GENRE

METHOD   LENGTH

NOTES/QUOTES

★★★★★

BOOK COVER

TITLE

AUTHOR

GENRE

METHOD   LENGTH

NOTES/QUOTES

★★★★★

BOOK COVER

TITLE

AUTHOR

GENRE

METHOD   LENGTH

NOTES/QUOTES

BOOK COVER

TITLE

AUTHOR

GENRE

METHOD   LENGTH

NOTES/QUOTES

BOOK COVER

TITLE
AUTHOR
GENRE
METHOD   LENGTH
NOTES/QUOTES

BOOK COVER

TITLE
AUTHOR
GENRE
METHOD   LENGTH
NOTES/QUOTES

BOOK COVER

TITLE
AUTHOR
GENRE
METHOD   LENGTH
NOTES/QUOTES

⭐⭐⭐⭐⭐

BOOK COVER

TITLE
AUTHOR
GENRE
METHOD   LENGTH
NOTES/QUOTES

⭐⭐⭐⭐⭐

BOOK COVER

TITLE
AUTHOR
GENRE
METHOD   LENGTH
NOTES/QUOTES

BOOK COVER

TITLE
AUTHOR
GENRE
METHOD   LENGTH
NOTES/QUOTES

BOOK COVER

TITLE
AUTHOR
GENRE
METHOD   LENGTH
NOTES/QUOTES

★★★★★

BOOK COVER

TITLE
AUTHOR
GENRE
METHOD   LENGTH
NOTES/QUOTES

★★★★★

BOOK COVER

TITLE
AUTHOR
GENRE
METHOD   LENGTH
NOTES/QUOTES

★ ★ ★ ★ ★

BOOK COVER

TITLE
AUTHOR
GENRE
METHOD   LENGTH
NOTES/QUOTES

★ ★ ★ ★ ★

BOOK COVER

TITLE
AUTHOR
GENRE
METHOD   LENGTH
NOTES/QUOTES

BOOK COVER

TITLE
AUTHOR
GENRE
METHOD   LENGTH
NOTES/QUOTES

BOOK COVER

TITLE
AUTHOR
GENRE
METHOD   LENGTH
NOTES/QUOTES

★★★★★

BOOK COVER

TITLE
AUTHOR
GENRE
METHOD   LENGTH
NOTES/QUOTES

★★★★★

BOOK COVER

TITLE

AUTHOR

GENRE

METHOD   LENGTH

NOTES/QUOTES

★★★★★

BOOK COVER

TITLE

AUTHOR

GENRE

METHOD   LENGTH

NOTES/QUOTES

★★★★★

BOOK COVER

TITLE
AUTHOR
GENRE
METHOD   LENGTH
NOTES/QUOTES

BOOK COVER

TITLE
AUTHOR
GENRE
METHOD   LENGTH
NOTES/QUOTES

BOOK COVER

TITLE
AUTHOR
GENRE
METHOD   LENGTH
NOTES/QUOTES

BOOK COVER

TITLE
AUTHOR
GENRE
METHOD   LENGTH
NOTES/QUOTES

BOOK COVER

TITLE
AUTHOR
GENRE
METHOD   LENGTH
NOTES/QUOTES

BOOK COVER

TITLE
AUTHOR
GENRE
METHOD   LENGTH
NOTES/QUOTES

BOOK COVER

TITLE
AUTHOR
GENRE
METHOD   LENGTH
NOTES/QUOTES

BOOK COVER

TITLE
AUTHOR
GENRE
METHOD   LENGTH
NOTES/QUOTES

BOOK COVER

TITLE
AUTHOR
GENRE
METHOD   LENGTH
NOTES/QUOTES

BOOK COVER

TITLE
AUTHOR
GENRE
METHOD   LENGTH
NOTES/QUOTES

BOOK COVER

TITLE

AUTHOR

GENRE

METHOD   LENGTH

NOTES/QUOTES

★ ★ ★ ★ ★

BOOK COVER

TITLE

AUTHOR

GENRE

METHOD   LENGTH

NOTES/QUOTES

★ ★ ★ ★ ★

BOOK COVER

TITLE

AUTHOR

GENRE

METHOD   LENGTH

NOTES/QUOTES

BOOK COVER

TITLE

AUTHOR

GENRE

METHOD   LENGTH

NOTES/QUOTES

BOOK COVER

TITLE

AUTHOR

GENRE

METHOD   LENGTH

NOTES/QUOTES

BOOK COVER

TITLE

AUTHOR

GENRE

METHOD   LENGTH

NOTES/QUOTES

BOOK COVER

TITLE
AUTHOR
GENRE
METHOD   LENGTH
NOTES/QUOTES

BOOK COVER

TITLE
AUTHOR
GENRE
METHOD   LENGTH
NOTES/QUOTES

BOOK COVER

TITLE
AUTHOR
GENRE
METHOD   LENGTH
NOTES/QUOTES

BOOK COVER

TITLE
AUTHOR
GENRE
METHOD   LENGTH
NOTES/QUOTES

BOOK COVER

TITLE

AUTHOR

GENRE

METHOD   LENGTH

NOTES/QUOTES

BOOK COVER

TITLE

AUTHOR

GENRE

METHOD   LENGTH

NOTES/QUOTES

BOOK COVER

TITLE

AUTHOR

GENRE

METHOD   LENGTH

NOTES/QUOTES

BOOK COVER

TITLE

AUTHOR

GENRE

METHOD   LENGTH

NOTES/QUOTES

BOOK COVER

TITLE

AUTHOR

GENRE

METHOD   LENGTH

NOTES/QUOTES

BOOK COVER

TITLE

AUTHOR

GENRE

METHOD   LENGTH

NOTES/QUOTES

BOOK COVER

TITLE

AUTHOR

GENRE

METHOD   LENGTH

NOTES/QUOTES

BOOK COVER

TITLE

AUTHOR

GENRE

METHOD   LENGTH

NOTES/QUOTES

BOOK COVER

TITLE
AUTHOR
GENRE
METHOD   LENGTH
NOTES/QUOTES

★ ★ ★ ★ ★

BOOK COVER

TITLE
AUTHOR
GENRE
METHOD   LENGTH
NOTES/QUOTES

★ ★ ★ ★ ★

BOOK COVER

TITLE

AUTHOR

GENRE

METHOD   LENGTH

NOTES/QUOTES

BOOK COVER

TITLE

AUTHOR

GENRE

METHOD   LENGTH

NOTES/QUOTES

BOOK COVER

TITLE _____

AUTHOR _____

GENRE _____

METHOD _____ **LENGTH** _____

NOTES/QUOTES

★ ★ ★ ★ ★

BOOK COVER

TITLE _____

AUTHOR _____

GENRE _____

METHOD _____ **LENGTH** _____

NOTES/QUOTES

★ ★ ★ ★ ★

BOOK COVER

TITLE
AUTHOR
GENRE
METHOD   LENGTH
NOTES/QUOTES

⭐⭐⭐⭐⭐

BOOK COVER

TITLE
AUTHOR
GENRE
METHOD   LENGTH
NOTES/QUOTES

⭐⭐⭐⭐⭐

BOOK COVER

TITLE

AUTHOR

GENRE

METHOD   LENGTH

NOTES/QUOTES

★★★★★

BOOK COVER

TITLE

AUTHOR

GENRE

METHOD   LENGTH

NOTES/QUOTES

★★★★★

BOOK COVER

TITLE

AUTHOR

GENRE

METHOD　　　　LENGTH

NOTES/QUOTES

★★★★★

BOOK COVER

TITLE

AUTHOR

GENRE

METHOD　　　　LENGTH

NOTES/QUOTES

★★★★★

BOOK COVER

TITLE _____

AUTHOR _____

GENRE _____

METHOD _____ **LENGTH** _____

NOTES/QUOTES

★ ★ ★ ★ ★

BOOK COVER

TITLE _____

AUTHOR _____

GENRE _____

METHOD _____ **LENGTH** _____

NOTES/QUOTES

★ ★ ★ ★ ★

BOOK COVER

TITLE

AUTHOR

GENRE

METHOD   LENGTH

NOTES/QUOTES

BOOK COVER

TITLE

AUTHOR

GENRE

METHOD   LENGTH

NOTES/QUOTES

BOOK COVER

TITLE

AUTHOR

GENRE

METHOD   LENGTH

NOTES/QUOTES

★★★★★

BOOK COVER

TITLE

AUTHOR

GENRE

METHOD   LENGTH

NOTES/QUOTES

★★★★★

BOOK COVER

TITLE

AUTHOR

GENRE

METHOD   LENGTH

NOTES/QUOTES

☆☆☆☆☆

BOOK COVER

TITLE

AUTHOR

GENRE

METHOD   LENGTH

NOTES/QUOTES

☆☆☆☆☆

BOOK COVER

TITLE

AUTHOR

GENRE

METHOD   LENGTH

NOTES/QUOTES

★★★★★

BOOK COVER

TITLE

AUTHOR

GENRE

METHOD   LENGTH

NOTES/QUOTES

★★★★★

BOOK COVER

TITLE
AUTHOR
GENRE
METHOD   LENGTH
NOTES/QUOTES

BOOK COVER

TITLE
AUTHOR
GENRE
METHOD   LENGTH
NOTES/QUOTES

BOOK COVER

TITLE
AUTHOR
GENRE
METHOD   LENGTH
NOTES/QUOTES

BOOK COVER

TITLE
AUTHOR
GENRE
METHOD   LENGTH
NOTES/QUOTES

BOOK COVER

TITLE _____

AUTHOR _____

GENRE _____

METHOD _____ **LENGTH** _____

NOTES/QUOTES

★ ★ ★ ★ ★

BOOK COVER

TITLE _____

AUTHOR _____

GENRE _____

METHOD _____ **LENGTH** _____

NOTES/QUOTES

★ ★ ★ ★ ★

BOOK COVER

TITLE

AUTHOR

GENRE

METHOD   LENGTH

NOTES/QUOTES

BOOK COVER

TITLE

AUTHOR

GENRE

METHOD   LENGTH

NOTES/QUOTES

BOOK COVER

TITLE
AUTHOR
GENRE
METHOD   LENGTH
NOTES/QUOTES

BOOK COVER

TITLE
AUTHOR
GENRE
METHOD   LENGTH
NOTES/QUOTES

BOOK COVER

TITLE
AUTHOR
GENRE
METHOD   LENGTH
NOTES/QUOTES

BOOK COVER

TITLE
AUTHOR
GENRE
METHOD   LENGTH
NOTES/QUOTES

BOOK COVER

TITLE

AUTHOR

GENRE

METHOD   LENGTH

NOTES/QUOTES

BOOK COVER

TITLE

AUTHOR

GENRE

METHOD   LENGTH

NOTES/QUOTES

BOOK COVER

TITLE

AUTHOR

GENRE

METHOD   LENGTH

NOTES/QUOTES

★★★★★

BOOK COVER

TITLE

AUTHOR

GENRE

METHOD   LENGTH

NOTES/QUOTES

★★★★★

BOOK COVER

TITLE _____

AUTHOR _____

GENRE _____

METHOD _____ LENGTH _____

NOTES/QUOTES

★ ★ ★ ★ ★

BOOK COVER

TITLE _____

AUTHOR _____

GENRE _____

METHOD _____ LENGTH _____

NOTES/QUOTES

★ ★ ★ ★ ★

BOOK COVER

TITLE
AUTHOR
GENRE
METHOD   LENGTH
NOTES/QUOTES

BOOK COVER

TITLE
AUTHOR
GENRE
METHOD   LENGTH
NOTES/QUOTES

BOOK COVER

TITLE _____

AUTHOR _____

GENRE _____

METHOD _____ LENGTH ____

NOTES/QUOTES

★ ★ ★ ★ ★

BOOK COVER

TITLE _____

AUTHOR _____

GENRE _____

METHOD _____ LENGTH ____

NOTES/QUOTES

★ ★ ★ ★ ★

BOOK COVER

TITLE
AUTHOR
GENRE
METHOD   LENGTH
NOTES/QUOTES

BOOK COVER

TITLE
AUTHOR
GENRE
METHOD   LENGTH
NOTES/QUOTES

BOOK COVER

TITLE

AUTHOR

GENRE

METHOD   LENGTH

NOTES/QUOTES

★★★★★

BOOK COVER

TITLE

AUTHOR

GENRE

METHOD   LENGTH

NOTES/QUOTES

★★★★★

BOOK COVER

TITLE

AUTHOR

GENRE

METHOD   LENGTH

NOTES/QUOTES

BOOK COVER

TITLE

AUTHOR

GENRE

METHOD   LENGTH

NOTES/QUOTES

BOOK COVER

TITLE
AUTHOR
GENRE
METHOD   LENGTH
NOTES/QUOTES

BOOK COVER

TITLE
AUTHOR
GENRE
METHOD   LENGTH
NOTES/QUOTES

BOOK COVER

★★★★★

TITLE

AUTHOR

GENRE

METHOD   LENGTH

NOTES/QUOTES

BOOK COVER

★★★★★

TITLE

AUTHOR

GENRE

METHOD   LENGTH

NOTES/QUOTES

BOOK COVER

TITLE _____

AUTHOR _____

GENRE _____

METHOD _____ **LENGTH** _____

NOTES/QUOTES

⭐⭐⭐⭐⭐

BOOK COVER

TITLE _____

AUTHOR _____

GENRE _____

METHOD _____ **LENGTH** _____

NOTES/QUOTES

⭐⭐⭐⭐⭐

BOOK COVER

TITLE
AUTHOR
GENRE
METHOD   LENGTH
NOTES/QUOTES

BOOK COVER

TITLE
AUTHOR
GENRE
METHOD   LENGTH
NOTES/QUOTES

BOOK COVER

TITLE

AUTHOR

GENRE

METHOD   LENGTH

NOTES/QUOTES

BOOK COVER

TITLE

AUTHOR

GENRE

METHOD   LENGTH

NOTES/QUOTES

BOOK COVER

TITLE

AUTHOR

GENRE

METHOD   LENGTH

NOTES/QUOTES

★★★★★

BOOK COVER

TITLE

AUTHOR

GENRE

METHOD   LENGTH

NOTES/QUOTES

★★★★★

BOOK COVER	TITLE
	AUTHOR
	GENRE
	METHOD　　　LENGTH
	NOTES/QUOTES

★ ★ ★ ★ ★

BOOK COVER	TITLE
	AUTHOR
	GENRE
	METHOD　　　LENGTH
	NOTES/QUOTES

★ ★ ★ ★ ★

BOOK COVER

TITLE

AUTHOR

GENRE

METHOD   LENGTH

NOTES/QUOTES

BOOK COVER

TITLE

AUTHOR

GENRE

METHOD   LENGTH

NOTES/QUOTES

BOOK COVER

TITLE
AUTHOR
GENRE
METHOD   LENGTH
NOTES/QUOTES

BOOK COVER

TITLE
AUTHOR
GENRE
METHOD   LENGTH
NOTES/QUOTES

BOOK COVER

TITLE
AUTHOR
GENRE
METHOD   LENGTH
NOTES/QUOTES

BOOK COVER

TITLE
AUTHOR
GENRE
METHOD   LENGTH
NOTES/QUOTES

BOOK COVER

TITLE
AUTHOR
GENRE
METHOD   LENGTH
NOTES/QUOTES

BOOK COVER

TITLE
AUTHOR
GENRE
METHOD   LENGTH
NOTES/QUOTES

BOOK COVER

TITLE

AUTHOR

GENRE

METHOD   LENGTH

NOTES/QUOTES

★★★★★

BOOK COVER

TITLE

AUTHOR

GENRE

METHOD   LENGTH

NOTES/QUOTES

★★★★★

BOOK COVER

TITLE

AUTHOR

GENRE

METHOD   LENGTH

NOTES/QUOTES

BOOK COVER

TITLE

AUTHOR

GENRE

METHOD   LENGTH

NOTES/QUOTES

BOOK COVER

TITLE
AUTHOR
GENRE
METHOD   LENGTH
NOTES/QUOTES

BOOK COVER

TITLE
AUTHOR
GENRE
METHOD   LENGTH
NOTES/QUOTES

BOOK COVER

TITLE
AUTHOR
GENRE
METHOD LENGTH
NOTES/QUOTES

★★★★★

BOOK COVER

TITLE
AUTHOR
GENRE
METHOD LENGTH
NOTES/QUOTES

★★★★★

BOOK COVER

TITLE

AUTHOR

GENRE

METHOD　　　LENGTH

NOTES/QUOTES

★★★★★

BOOK COVER

TITLE

AUTHOR

GENRE

METHOD　　　LENGTH

NOTES/QUOTES

★★★★★

BOOK COVER

TITLE

AUTHOR

GENRE

METHOD   LENGTH

NOTES/QUOTES

BOOK COVER

TITLE

AUTHOR

GENRE

METHOD   LENGTH

NOTES/QUOTES

BOOK COVER

TITLE

AUTHOR

GENRE

METHOD   LENGTH

NOTES/QUOTES

★★★★★

BOOK COVER

TITLE

AUTHOR

GENRE

METHOD   LENGTH

NOTES/QUOTES

★★★★★

BOOK COVER

TITLE
AUTHOR
GENRE
METHOD   LENGTH
NOTES/QUOTES

BOOK COVER

TITLE
AUTHOR
GENRE
METHOD   LENGTH
NOTES/QUOTES

BOOK COVER

TITLE

AUTHOR

GENRE

METHOD   LENGTH

NOTES/QUOTES

BOOK COVER

TITLE

AUTHOR

GENRE

METHOD   LENGTH

NOTES/QUOTES

BOOK COVER

TITLE

AUTHOR

GENRE

METHOD   LENGTH

NOTES/QUOTES

BOOK COVER

TITLE

AUTHOR

GENRE

METHOD   LENGTH

NOTES/QUOTES

BOOK COVER

TITLE
AUTHOR
GENRE
METHOD   LENGTH
NOTES/QUOTES

BOOK COVER

TITLE
AUTHOR
GENRE
METHOD   LENGTH
NOTES/QUOTES

BOOK COVER

TITLE
AUTHOR
GENRE
METHOD   LENGTH
NOTES/QUOTES

BOOK COVER

TITLE
AUTHOR
GENRE
METHOD   LENGTH
NOTES/QUOTES

BOOK COVER

TITLE

AUTHOR

GENRE

METHOD   LENGTH

NOTES/QUOTES

BOOK COVER

TITLE

AUTHOR

GENRE

METHOD   LENGTH

NOTES/QUOTES

BOOK COVER

TITLE

AUTHOR

GENRE

METHOD   LENGTH

NOTES/QUOTES

BOOK COVER

TITLE

AUTHOR

GENRE

METHOD   LENGTH

NOTES/QUOTES

BOOK COVER

TITLE

AUTHOR

GENRE

METHOD   LENGTH

NOTES/QUOTES

BOOK COVER

TITLE

AUTHOR

GENRE

METHOD   LENGTH

NOTES/QUOTES

BOOK COVER

TITLE
AUTHOR
GENRE
METHOD   LENGTH
NOTES/QUOTES

★★★★★

BOOK COVER

TITLE
AUTHOR
GENRE
METHOD   LENGTH
NOTES/QUOTES

★★★★★